THE BACKYARD LANDSCAPER

40 Professional Designs for Do-It-Yourselfers

Created by
Susan A. Roth & Company

Landscape Designs by
Ireland-Gannon Associates, Inc.

Project Managers:
Michael J. Opisso and **Damon Scott**

Landscape Illustrations by
Ray Skibinski

 **HOME PLANNERS, INC.**

Designed and Produced by: Susan A. Roth & Company
3 Lamont Lane
Stony Brook, NY 11790

Publisher: Susan A. Roth
Associate Editor: Pam Peirce
Copy Editor: Susan Lang
Writers: Cathy W. Barash, Ann Reilly, Susan A. Roth, and
Mark Schneider

Landscape designs by: Ireland-Gannon Associates, Inc.
Rt 25A, Northern Blvd.
East Norwich, NY 11732

Damon Scott   Tom Nordloh
Michael J. Opisso   Jim Morgan
David Poplawski

Regional consultants:
Northeast: Carol Howe
Mid-Atlantic: Michael J. Opisso
Deep South: Nancy Jacobs Roney
Midwest: Ruth Kvaalen
Florida and Gulf Coast: Robert Haehle
Rocky Mountains: Allen M. Wilson

Northern California and Pacific Northwest:
   Jo Wilson Greenstreet
Southern California and Desert Southwest:
   Margaret West
Regional Map Consultant: Pam Elum

Artwork by:
Landscape Renderings: Ray Skibinski
Landscape Plot Plans: Damon Scott and Michael Iragorri
How-To Artwork: Ron Hildebrand
Compost Bin: Frank Fretz (color); Carson Ode (how-to)

Photographs by:
Susan A. Roth: cover, title, 6, 9, 11, 13, 15, 18, 19B, 20, 32, 34, 46, 48, 60, 70, 72, 73, 86, 98, 112, 114, 115, 124, 126, 136, 145
Carl Saporiti: 8, 10, 12, 14, 16, 100, Karen Bussolini: 22, 84
David Poplawski: 19T, 58, Judith Carlson: 142, David Goldberg: 138
Cover photo: Landscape Design by Conni Cross, Landscape Designer, Cutchogue, NY; Stonework by Dan Messina, Mason,
Manorville, NY.

Published by Home Planners, Inc.

Editorial and Corporate Office:
   3275 West Ina Road, Suite 110
   Tucson, AZ 85741
Distribution Center:
   29333 Lorie Lane
   Wixom, MI 48393

Chairman: Charles W. Talcott
President and Publisher: Rickard D. Bailey
Publications Manager: Cindy Coatsworth
Editor: Paulette Mulvin
Book Designer: Paul Fitzgerald

10 9 8 7 6 5 4 3 2 1

Library of Congress Catalogue Card Number: 91-073385
ISBN softcover: 0-918894-89-1
ISBN hardcover: 0-918894-92-1

CONTENTS

INTRODUCTION

Your backyard is your family's private outdoor living space. With thoughtful planning, it can be arranged any way that meets your particular needs. This book will help you fulfill your yard's potential to become a lovely retreat, a special place to enjoy outdoor hobbies and gardening activities, or an inviting locale for entertaining and relaxing. You'll learn that there's no right or wrong way to design a backyard and no need to match a particular style of architecture, because your backyard is your private gardening and recreation space.

The Backyard Landscaper is an unusual book. Here you'll find plot plans and illustrations of professionally designed backyards for which you can order actual customized blueprints. You can choose to order a full-size, six-page blueprint package complete with a regionalized plant list selected for your area — or you can use what you see here as an inspiration for creating your own distinctive landscape.

This unique idea is the result of the collaboration of three talented companies: Home Planners, Inc., architects and publishers of blueprints for do-it-yourself home builders and contractors; Susan A. Roth & Company, a horticultural publishing and book packaging company; and Ireland-Gannon Associates, Inc., a nationally recognized, award-winning, landscape design-build firm. These companies are tops in their fields.

Home Planners, Inc. was founded in 1946 and has published more than one hundred and thirty-five books of home plans, and sold more than two and a half million blueprints for its designs. Its home plans are featured regularly in special issues of *House Beautiful, Better Homes and Gardens, Colonial Homes*, and other leading shelter magazines. Its first book of landscape plans, *The Home Landscaper*, offers designs for 40 front yard and 15 backyard landscapes.

Susan A. Roth & Company created *The Home Landscaper* for Home Planners and has put together many popular gardening books for Ortho Books. The author of *The Weekend Garden Guide — Work-Saving Ways to a Beautiful Backyard* (Rodale Press, 1991) and a contributor to many publications,

Susan A. Roth is also a widely published garden photographer who maintains a large slide library.

Ireland-Gannon Associates, Inc. has served the prestigious North Shore of Long Island since 1943. In 1978, the company formed an association with the acclaimed Martin Viette Nursery, a major horticultural center in the Northeast. Ireland-Gannon has been honored with more than forty awards in the last 20 years, including several Grand Awards from the Associated Landscape Contractors of America and Superior Awards from the National Landscape Association.

By using the designs in the book, you'll have an alternative to hiring a landscape architect or landscape designer to create a backyard plan for you. Most top-notch firms charge between $500 and $1,000 to design the planting scheme for a ½-acre property. For a fraction of that cost, you can order from this book a large professional-quality blueprint package tailored to your needs. Each package comes in eight regionalized versions featuring planting schemes coded with plants specially selected to thrive in various parts of the United States and Canada. (See page 156.)

ABOUT THE DESIGNS IN THIS BOOK

Horticulturists and landscape designers have combined their talents to create 40 professional-quality backyard landscape designs for do-it-yourselfers and landscape contractors. The plans offer a range of possibilities for small or large families and for compact or spacious lots. The plans are organized into nine themed chapters to meet the needs of most families.

Because many people have difficulty imagining what a one-dimensional planting plan will look like in reality, a full-color illustration accompanies each plot plan. This image shows the landscape after it has matured and filled in to give you a sense of the mood and feeling the landscape design will invoke a few years after it's installed.

In the first chapter, you'll read about what makes a successful landscape design. This will help you appreciate the intentions of the designs in the ensuing

4

chapters and will assist you in modifying the plans if need be. The information in the chapter will also be helpful if you decide to do your own design.

In Chapter 2, you can read about how to create a backyard for children to play in. Children need room to run, hide, and jump — all the activities that come under the category of play. Children will play whether your garden accounts for their needs or not. In a backyard designed to accommodate them, they'll have a safer place to romp and will be less likely to upset the order of things.

Chapter 3 includes five different naturalistic gardens. Of course, what is natural depends in large measure on the environment where you live. That's why the plans offered here include a meadow garden, shade garden, rock garden, water garden, and woodland wildflower walk. Look for one that suits your taste and your surroundings.

Perhaps the most practical backyard of all is one that produces something you and your family can eat. That's the theme of Chapter 4: "Backyards for Food Gardeners." Four plans are presented to meet the needs of any backyard food gardener.

Turn to Chapter 5 if you either have or desire a backyard with a swimming pool. The plans span a spectrum of styles: a naturalistic pool resembling a small pond; a lap pool for exercising in a limited space; a kidney-shaped pool for an elegant look; and a pool with a spacious deck for gala pool parties.

If you want to have a beautiful backyard but don't have a lot of time to devote to it, check the plans in Chapter 6, "Low-Maintenance Backyard Designs." Five different approaches are illustrated. All have these features in common: The plants are types that require little attention from you; the lawn is kept small with few edges to trim; and the trees and shrubs are slow-growing or dwarf types that fit into the landscape without requiring regular pruning.

If you're the type of gardener who wants to have an abundance of flowers to tend or to cut and bring indoors, turn to Chapter 7, where you'll discover several backyard designs for the flower gardener. You'll find a variety of backyard plans featuring specialty flower gardens.

For many homeowners, the backyard represents an extension of their living space — a place to relax or entertain outdoors. If your idea of paradise is a barbecue or a hammock, or if you see your yard as the perfect place to host a wedding reception, turn to Chapter 8, "Backyards for Outdoor Living."

Chapter 9, "Backyards to Attract Wildlife," features several backyard plans to bring birds and butterflies into your yard. One of the greatest contributions home gardeners can make to the health of their local environment is a garden that provides food, water, and shelter for wildlife.

Chapter 10, "Picturesque Flower Garden Designs," will be the most useful chapter of all for many readers. It contains four plans for intricate flower gardens rather than entire backyards. You can implement these plans just as they are or you can adapt them, whether you're starting to landscape your property or have a long-established one in need of renovation.

HOW TO USE THIS BOOK

The first chapter of this book provides some basic information about backyard landscaping. You'll read about the design principles that professional landscapers put into practice. Then browse through Chapters 2 through 10 — the plot plans and illustrations of various gardens that are the heart of this book. When you study them, you'll see how the principles discussed in Chapter 1 are used to create truly useful and attractive landscapes.

If you would like to install any of these landscapes on your property, use the plot plan provided in the book to guide you, modifying it if necessary to fit the exact contours of your house and property. It isn't necessary to order the blueprint package offered with each design; however, the six-page package contains enlarged, easy-to-use blueprints, a regionalized plant list selected especially for your climate, as well as several pages of information on planting and caring for your new landscape.

Chapter 11 tells you how to work with the landscape plans shown here and helps you through the installation process, whether you choose to do the work yourself or hire a landscape contractor to do the construction and planting.

Chapter 12 is a sort of appendix covering a number of practical and aesthetic features that can enhance any garden. Here you'll find examples of gazebos, tool sheds, decks, compost bins, birdhouses, and other garden structures that you can build yourself or buy in kit form.

INSTALLING THE LANDSCAPE

Most do-it-yourselfers can install any of these landscapes themselves. If you don't want to do the construction or planting personally, you can hire a landscape contractor — a professional installer — to do the job. Keep in mind that most landscape contractors aren't skilled designers, even though they may promote themselves as such. Their skills lie in maintaining a lawn, planting or removing trees, or regrading the land, but when it comes to actual landscape design their talents may be limited. You can be assured of getting a top-quality landscape if you start with a plan from this book — one created by an award-winning landscape design firm — and then, if you wish, hire a skilled contractor to install it. Landscaping is an investment in the enjoyment and value of your home, so why not begin with the best design possible?

Landscape design: Mitsuka Collver

Here's a prescription for a backyard paradise: a garden pond complete with waterlilies, borders brimming with perennials, flowering shrubs and ornamental trees, and an inviting patio where you can sit and enjoy it all.

LANDSCAPE YOUR BACKYARD THE PROFESSIONAL WAY

Learn the Landscape Principles and Techniques Professionals Use

Y ou've been in your new house for several weeks now: Maybe it has just been built and is standing on an empty lot, or perhaps it's an older home with trees and shrubs already established. Or maybe you've been living in your home for years, waiting for the kids to arrive — or to leave — before you fix up the yard. Whatever the circumstances, now you have the desire and the wherewithal to make your backyard the attractive outdoor environment you want it to be. But do you know how to begin? Do you have the confidence to design your own landscape? Can you afford to hire a professional landscape architect or garden designer? If you answer "no" to these questions, this book, which will help you do it all by yourself, may be just the answer you've been looking for.

A landscape professional would ask you some important questions before beginning any type of design, but you can go through the process by yourself with the help of this book. Ask yourself these questions, writing down your answers and making lists if you wish.

- Who will use the backyard, when, and for what purposes?
- Which backyard features are most important to you and your family?
- How much time do you have to tend the yard?
- What are the growing conditions in the yard?

Consider whether or not you want your backyard

to be a playground for children, an outdoor dining room, or a picturesque scene to view from a window or a deck. Do you want to grow flowers for arranging, or fruits and vegetables to fill the freezer? Does your family long for a pool to swim in and relax by? Once you know what you want, you can select one of the professionally designed plans in this book. It's almost as good as having a plan custom-made for your family. If you wish, you can order large, detailed blueprints with a regionalized plant list for any of the 40 backyard designs featured in this book. (See page 154 for ordering information.)

ORGANIZING THE SPACES IN YOUR BACKYARD

Landscape designers know that to enjoy your property to the fullest, it's best to organize the outdoor spaces in the backyard in ways that fulfill many of the same basic needs as the rooms in a house. As with the indoors, the backyard should have areas where your family can relax, play, entertain, cook, and dine. You may also want places for storage and pursuing outdoor hobbies, such as vegetable or flower gardening. And, as with the interior decor, the backyard decor will be most enjoyable and inviting if it offers an attractive and private environment of pleasing colors and textures.

Creating a total landscape design is similar in some ways to decorating an interior. As you study the backyard plans in this book, try to think of the landscape as consisting of floors, walls, and ceilings,

Landscape design: Ireland-Gannon Associates

just as the rooms in a house do. The main difference is that the basic elements — floors, walls, and ceilings — are created and enhanced with plants and construction elements, such as fences, patios, and paths.

Creating Garden Floors

The lawn, other low-growing plants used as a ground cover, and construction materials, such as wood, concrete, brick, flagstone, gravel, and wood chips, create the outdoor floors. Before making any decision about which types of flooring to use in various locations in your backyard, think about how much use each area will receive and how the pavement or plants fit into the rest of the landscape design. A professional designer considers the colors and textures of these elements before making a final decision and, where possible, uses construction materials for walkways, decks, and patios that match the construction of the house. This creates unity in the landscape.

A lawn forms the floor for the major part of most backyards. A large lawn fits many design styles except perhaps a woodland, desert, or Mediterranean landscape. You'll probably want a lawn as a floor for recreation areas where kids will be playing games or sports because grass is softer, cooler, and more resilient than paving or wood, creating a safe place to frolic. In addition, a lawn feels good under bare feet. A green lawn also forms an important element of a design — its fine texture and color tie the diverse parts of a landscape together, setting off bolder-textured and more brightly colored plants.

Most backyards need a hard-surfaced floor within easy access of the house in an area intended for

barbecuing, dining, and entertaining because the hard surface will hold up better during heavy use. This floor defines the area and boundaries of the garden room intended for outdoor living.

The size and shape of a patio or deck depend on the family's needs and the size of the property. A professional designer will include a large patio or deck to occupy a major portion of the backyard only if it fits into the overall design and scale of the property. Even then, the designer will balance the visual weight of the area with an equally weighty planting of trees and shrubs.

Walkways, like hallways, should be wide enough to permit easy access and surfaced with a material that's easy to walk on without slipping. The material chosen for the walk must match the rest of the hardscape or complement the landscape style. For instance, brick is appropriate in a formal herb garden, whereas wood chips are more in keeping with a woodland wildflower path.

Ground covers like English ivy or pachysandra work wonders in covering large areas that don't get heavy foot traffic. A low ground cover, such as wintercreeper or prostrate juniper, provides a bolder texture than lawn and can be used to sculpt beautiful curves or cover shady ground where grass won't grow well. Because ground covers are low, they don't block views. Although ground covers are part of the garden floor, they act somewhat like low walls since they tend to direct where people walk.

As you'll note when studying the designs in this book, a floor of ground covers is the best way to unite a shrub border and connect two separate areas of the landscape. A ground cover of vinca, for instance, creates a tapestry of foliage and flowers beneath masses of shrubbery just as a fine Oriental carpet sets off the furniture in a study. Once a ground cover fills in, it keeps out weeds and shades and cools the soil, thus reducing maintenance and improving the health of the shrubs.

Creating Garden Walls

Hedges, shrubbery, and constructed walls and fences act as outdoor walls, serving many landscape functions. They define boundaries, separate one garden area from another, provide privacy from neighbors, and block unsightly views. Walls become especially important for creating privacy in suburban backyards if you don't want your neighbors sharing your outdoor living space with you.

Constructed walls can be wood or metal fences or sturdy brick, stone, or masonry walls. As with flooring materials, walls look best when they reflect the building materials or style of the house. A wall should serve a purpose in the landscape. Used to border a small garden or courtyard, a rock or brick wall creates a sense of intimacy and enclosure. A constructed wall also makes an effective background for a flower garden or a low shrub border. A tall wall provides shade and can help to slow a wind. Low walls separate different garden areas and direct traffic without restricting views. Although a low wall often proves to be more decorative than useful, it can double as a garden seat or bear planters of flowers. See page 13 for more information about constructed walls.

Consider all the shrubbery in your landscape — whether it consists of formal clipped hedges or informal free-flowing masses — as part of the walls of the landscape. Unlike a constructed wall, a living wall can provide flowers, fragrance, berries, fall foliage color, or a home for birds. Plants with thorns or sharp leaves, such as barberry, holly, and pyracantha, make useful security barriers.

Where the landscape walls need to provide year-round privacy, evergreen shrubs are the answer. Evergreens can be used to create permanent barriers from neighboring properties or from an adjoining street. In addition, evergreen plants provide shelter for birds in winter.

Deciduous shrubs also make effective walls, since their thick foliage provides privacy during the warm-weather months when your family uses the yard the most. Many deciduous shrubs, such as spirea, weigela, and viburnum, bloom during spring and summer, providing an abundance of eye-level blossoms.

Creating Garden Ceilings

Although the sky actually forms the principal ceiling of a landscape, trees and overhead structures add to the ceiling of the created landscape. By partially blocking the expanse of sky, trees and structures frame and enhance the overhead view, setting off a sunset or fluffy white clouds on a summer afternoon. Garden ceilings provide relief from the hot summer sun or a heavy rain, as well as create beauty overhead and interesting shadow patterns on the ground.

Tall shade trees and smaller canopy trees form the primary garden ceilings, casting welcome shade on a backyard sitting area or a playground. Trees also create a beautiful overhead structure and add

Separating the front of the property from the backyard, a gate and vine-covered lattice fence form the door and walls of this outdoor room, creating an inviting and private space.

Landscape design: Conni Cross

9

By connecting directly to sliding glass doors leading to the interior of the house, the expansive deck greatly increases the home's living space.

Landscape design: Ireland-Gannon Associates

strength to the landscape design. When choosing shade trees, select ones with interesting silhouettes, colorful fall foliage, or attractive flowers. Many trees also have characteristic shapes that lend themselves to certain garden styles. Linden trees and Bradford pears have uniform oval shapes that go well with formal landscape designs, whereas red oaks and crab apples grow into irregular and chunky shapes befitting more informal backyards.

When working with existing trees, you may wish to prune off the lower branches to provide clearance for sitting or dining. You may also want to selectively remove branches from mature trees to allow more light to penetrate to the shrubs and flowers below.

Vines can create ceilings when they're grown on overhead structures. When vines are allowed to twine through trellises and arbors, they beautify and shade a sitting area on a patio or deck. Hanging baskets of trailing annual flowers, such as nasturtium or verbena, suspended overhead from an arbor brighten the area for months on end and visually tie the floor and ceiling together.

A PLACE FOR RELAXING AND ENTERTAINING OUTDOORS

Every backyard needs a place to relax and entertain outdoors — a place where you can extend your indoor living to the outdoors. Landscaping experts feel that the relaxation area should stand alone functionally, yet blend with the rest of the landscaping around your home. A patio, deck, terrace, or barbecuing area is most convenient if it's located on the same level as and within easy access of the house, especially the kitchen. But if a better spot exists, such as one with a magnificent view, a second sitting area can

be located there as well. Sliding glass or French doors leading to a patio or deck tie indoors and outdoors together, enhancing the view and traffic flow.

Since the primary outdoor relaxation area will get heavy use, the floor shouldn't consist of lawn but rather a construction material. It should be large enough to accommodate a table, lounge chairs, a barbecue, and the typical number of people you intend to entertain. If you plan large outdoor parties, provide a paved surface big enough for all your guests to stand and mingle comfortably. The Formal Garden for Entertaining (L243 on page 108), for example, provides ample room for large parties. All too often, builders include only a tiny patio, one that has barely enough room to hold all family members, much less guests.

When siting a deck or patio, you can work with the existing trees and topography as long as you don't change the soil level around tree roots — to do so would probably kill them. Setting a deck or patio in the shade of an existing tree visually anchors the landscape and makes for a comfortable spot to relax on hot afternoons. If a sitting area is situated in a wooded area away from the house, the pathway and steps leading to it can be made to twist and turn through the trees, creating a walk-in-the-woods feeling. You can place a brick patio under a large specimen tree — a circular pattern looks quite attractive — and add a circular bench around the tree trunk. Similarly, a deck can be built with a well and a bench and even a table surrounding the trunk, such as in the Backyard Meadow Garden (see Plan L258 on page 36).

Outdoor living areas work well when they connect with the indoors, forming an extension of the house.

When a patio or deck can be reached from sliding glass or French doors that open off the dining room, living room, or kitchen, the outdoor space becomes an extension of that room, creating a flowing space for entertaining. Attaching latticework to the house and extending it over the deck or patio not only creates shade but makes a visual connection between the patio and the house.

If the land slopes away from the house, an area below can be leveled and connected to the house with a series of wide steps and platforms. Another way to increase usable space in a sloped backyard is to cantilever a deck over the slope, such as in the Second-Story Deck (see Plan L249 on page 110), thereby creating a spot for enjoying the view below. It's also possible to fill in a sloped area and hold it in place with a retaining wall.

SELECTING THE PERFECT HARDSCAPE FOR YOUR OUTDOOR LIVING SCAPE

The paving, fences, walls, and garden ornaments used in a landscape design are often called the hardscape, whereas the plant materials are referred to as the softscape. The hardscape plays an important role in your backyard design. Well-designed landscapes use paving materials whose color, texture, and pattern complement the construction material of the house.

INSTALLING WALKWAYS

Walkways provide ease of movement from one area of the garden to another. They also provide a feeling of continuity, especially if the same paving material used at the entry leads to the side yard and the backyard.

Landscape designers are careful that the lines of the walk don't cut the design so much that the property seems choppy or smaller than it really is. The landscape designs presented here demonstrate that a straight line may be the shortest distance between two points but it's not necessarily the best landscaping principle. Only in formal gardens are walkways straight. Curved pathways are attractive, and they can be used to block views, giving the feeling that they're leading to something special beyond and making the property appear larger.

When a material like flagstone is used, the stones can be laid so that the edges of the walkway are irregular to fit in with an informal design. In natural settings, the walks and paths can be paved with wood chips, pine needles, crushed stone,

Stepping-stones look more informal and less weighty than a solid walk, yet serve effectively to protect the lawn while directing people through the garden. Here, the stone pavers of the walk are repeated as an edging for the brick patio, creating a cohesive design.

Landscape design: Ireland-Gannon Associates

11

Landscape design: Ireland-Gannon Associates

A brick patio and pool edging, stepping-stone walk, and even the round table and umbrella create a wonderful repeating pattern of smooth curves that brings a peaceful feeling to this backyard.

crushed seashells, or gravel. These materials should be used only on flat or almost flat areas since they can wash away on slopes.

Stepping-stones laid through a lawn create an informal walk to direct people to a door, gate, or special garden site. Less weighty and more casual than a paved walk, the stepping-stones will still protect the lawn from excessive wear and tear in heavily traveled areas.

Make sure a walkway can accommodate the intended number of people walking abreast and that it's wide enough for maintenance equipment.

Building Patios and Decks

Brick is frequently used to pave a patio or terrace, although concrete, concrete pavers, stone, and other materials may be used. Also suitable for driveways, walkways, and steps, bricks are available in different textures and colors. Smooth-finished bricks look beautiful in a patio; used bricks are rougher in texture and, therefore, more appropriate for walkways. Common brick patterns include running bond, basket weave, herringbone, pinwheel, and circular. The different patterns have different textures and moods, some more formal and others more casual. When laying a brick walk that turns sharply or meets a brick patio, the direction of the pattern can change to indicate a turn or transition.

A common brick measures 3¾ by 8 by 2¼ inches. Other types include Roman brick, which measures

1½ by 4 by 12 inches, and paving brick, which is 3½ by 4 by 8 inches. Bricks embedded in mortar or concrete have more permanence and resist weeds better; however, bricks can be laid in a 2-inch base of sand, as long as an automobile won't be driven over them. If the soil doesn't drain well or your area has severely cold winters, lay 3 to 5 inches of crushed rock under the sand. After you arrange the bricks in a pattern, brush more sand on top until the cracks are filled.

Concrete is one of the most inexpensive paving materials, although not always the most attractive. It can be laid in any shape and may be the easiest way to deal with a circle. Smooth concrete is slippery when wet; a textured finish is safer and can be made more attractive with a sweeping circular design. Adding heavy aggregate to concrete strengthens it and makes it more attractive, as does dividing it into sections bordered by strips of treated wood. Concrete can also be beautified by coloring it, stamping it in various patterns or shapes, or topping it with colored stones.

Precast interlocking concrete pavers, which are strong and easy to install, come in a variety of shapes, textures, and colors. Although more expensive than concrete, they're more economical than brick or stones like slate or flagstone. Quarried stones, including granite, marble, bluestone, and slate, are often used as paving materials for patios and walks. Since dimensioned stone is cut, it's easy to work with because it's usually even. Fieldstone can also be used, but you'll have to find relatively flat stones and bury them partway so that the surface is level and easy to walk on.

Decks are almost always built with durable redwood, cedar, or cypress. Pressure-treated lumber, which is usually a preservative-treated pine or Douglas fir, endures better than any of the other woods and should be used where the structure comes in contact with the soil, although it's not as attractive for finished surfaces. It's slightly green when new, but it weathers naturally to a light gray and doesn't need painting or staining.

Decks are usually raised to meet the level of the house to avoid stepping down. This necessitates steps leading to the ground level and railings for safety. Railings should be designed carefully as they're an integral part of the structure. They must also meet local building requirements for strength and safety. They should be strong enough to sit on or lean against, and the design should preclude a small child climbing over the top or squeezing through the supports.

Selecting Wall and Fence Materials

Walls can be made of stone, brick, wood, concrete, or adobe. Stone is more expensive than brick, but it's quite durable and fits well into a country-style or farmhouse landscape. Fieldstone makes excellent dry walls, which can be accented or softened with plants growing between the stones. Railroad ties and landscape timbers are often used for constructing retaining walls, edgings, and the sides of raised planters.

Authentic railroad ties measure 8 to 10 feet long and have variable heights and widths; they're usually treated with creosote, a preservative toxic to people and plants. Landscape timbers are generally made of pressure-treated lumber and are 8 feet long and either 6 by 6, 6 by 8, or 8 by 8 inches around. They're preferable owing to their nontoxicity, longevity, and uniformity.

Low brick or stone retaining walls are often used to change the grade. They look striking built into a slope and filled in behind with topsoil, thus adding height and contour to the landscape. When a retaining wall is constructed, it must be angled back into the fill behind it for stability. A low retaining wall can be planted with flowers, ground covers, or low shrubs that hug the top of the wall and cascade over it, softening the appearance of the stone or brick.

Fences provide privacy in most backyards. Usually made of wood or metal, they come in many styles that can contribute to the landscape design. Wood fences should be constructed of redwood, cedar, or cypress, since these woods are the most weather resistant. Pressure-treated lumber makes long-lasting posts, since it resists rot. Chainlink fences work in areas where children or pets need to be confined, and around swimming pools because they allow you

Landscape design: Conni Cross

While serving the practical purpose of changing the grade, this stone retaining wall serves an aesthetic function by creating a lovely setting for displaying flowers and shrubs.

to see through them while still providing security. Chainlink is more durable than wood, although not as attractive. The appeal of this kind of fence can be heightened by using chainlink coated with green or black vinyl, or by hiding the fence with vines or shrubs.

When planning a wall or fence, consider its height in relationship to the property's needs for privacy and security. (Local zoning regulations usually limit height.) In some cases, the type of boundary fences used within a neighborhood should be considered so the garden wall blends with surrounding properties. Be sure to make any gates wide enough to accommodate a lawn mower and other maintenance equipment.

PROFESSIONAL LANDSCAPE DESIGN TECHNIQUES

If you took the time to analyze the characteristics of the professionally designed landscapes in this book, you would see many similarities. Although each

Landscape design: Ireland-Gannon Associates

garden is unique, they all work because they have certain aesthetic principles in common. The basic design principles described here will help you interpret the landscape designs in this book and teach you to create an effective design of your own.

Drawing the Line

The overall contours of the hardscape and the softscape of a yard create the design's lines. These lines may be curved or straight, horizontal or vertical. When repeated and contrasted, they give the landscape visual harmony and excitement. The choice of line depends on the size of your garden space and the architectural style of your house and landscape.

Curved lines have a freer, more natural feeling than straight lines, which seem more formal and quiet. Vertical lines give strength, and horizontal lines imply permanence and flow. Squares and rectangles are formal, whereas circles and curves are more informal. Oblique angles suggest power and boldness, although too many different angles appear weak and distracting. Most good landscape designs balance the horizontal and vertical lines.

The lines of a landscape direct the viewer's eye, focusing interest on particular parts of the landscape. The lines may be continuous or broken, although there must be no visual stop when they're broken; instead, your eye should be able to pick up the continuity from one section of the design to another. This helps create harmony.

Experienced designers manipulate the lines in a garden to please and trick the eye: They may contour a flower bed to make a narrow part of the garden seem wider, or they may design a hedge with a path that disappears past it to make a small yard seem larger.

Using Form and Shape

The three-dimensional shapes of a landscape are its forms. Plants may be upright, spreading, arching, weeping, rounded, columnar, pyramidal, or irregular in form. The overall form of a well-designed garden results from combining and repeating plant forms that balance and complement each other.

Too many forms alternating with one another are busy and visually disturbing. It is more pleasing to group similarly shaped plants using a contrasting shape for accent. Combining several plants of the same type to create a mass of flower color and foliage texture is a frequently used technique for giving a design impact.

Understanding Texture, From Fine to Coarse

The surface of a plant or any other landscape material has a texture that catches the eye. Plants are considered fine, medium, or coarse textured depending on their leaf size and the circumference of their branches. For instance, boxwood, which has tiny, oval leaves, is fine textured and calm, whereas rhododendron, with its large, oblong leaves, appears coarse textured and bold.

Texture also implies weight. Plants with stiff branches or rough, coarse, large, or dull foliage appear heavier and have more substance than plants with loose branches and smooth, fine, or glossy foliage.

Knowing how to effectively combine and contrast textures is one of the most important skills of a good landscape designer. Using too many contrasting textures together tends to create an overly busy feeling. On the other hand, too much sameness, whether from fine- or bold-textured materials, can be boring and static. Plant textures should harmonize with features of the hardscape and vice versa.

Landscape designers sometimes use texture to create illusions. Fine-textured plants appear farther away than they really are, whereas large-textured plants appear closer and are more exciting. You can make small spaces feel roomier with fine-textured plants and large areas more intimate by planting coarse-textured plants in the distance, thus creating the illusion that they're closer than they actually are.

Creating Color Harmony and Contrast

We automatically think of flowers when discussing garden color, but color comes from more than flowers. Consider the color of foliage, berries, bark, and construction materials when designing your garden. Leaves may be various shades of green, from gray-green to yellow-green to grass green, or they may be deep burgundy or golden yellow. Some plants feature green leaves variegated with white or yellow; some change to red, yellow, or bronze in fall, and others remain green the year around. And, of course, paving and other construction materials contribute color to the landscape. Brick has an especially strong color that should be considered carefully when you design the color scheme of your backyard.

Color elicits a strong emotional appeal and influences a landscape design in many ways. Repetition of color creates a pleasing pattern and visual unity within the design. Masses of the same flowering plant make a bold statement. A mixture of many different colors dissipates unity and seems weak. You can also use color to lead the eye to various landscape accents and focal points.

Colors can be categorized as warm or cool. Red, orange, and yellow seem as warm as the sun, whereas blue, green, and violet seem as cool as ice. Warm colors tend to advance visually, becoming more stimulating and aggressive than cool colors, which tend to recede and loose their impact when viewed from a distance. Cool colors make good accents and look best in a relatively small space near a sitting area. Or they can be used in a small garden to

Top right: Many ornamental trees, such as birch, feature brilliant fall foliage color and decorative bark for year-round appeal. Center right: Flowers, such as hydrangea, contribute outstanding color to a landscape. Bottom right: Gleaming berries, as from pyracantha, offer landscape color in fall and winter.

Several large island beds of narrow-trunked trees create masses of overhead foliage that cast a pleasing shade across the lawn while balancing the visual weight of the house and deck.

Landscape design: Ireland-Gannon Associates

make it feel larger, whereas using warm colors in the same garden will make the area seem smaller. It's best to decide on one dominant color and combine it with smaller amounts of one or two other colors to create a pleasing color scheme.

When combining colors you can use color wheel harmonies with good effect. Complementary colors are opposite each other on the color wheel — for example, red and blue, or yellow and violet. Analogous color harmony uses colors that are adjacent on the color wheel — for example, yellow and orange, or blue and violet. Monochromatic harmony relies on different tints and shades of the same color, such as you would see in an all-pink or all-blue garden.

Using Pattern and Rhythm

Effective landscape designs relate each part of a garden to its other parts with a recognizable pattern. The arrangement and use of textures, colors, and forms within the landscape create patterns. The pattern may be a naturalistic or stylized arrangement. Repetition of pattern throughout a landscape or garden proves essential to the movement and rhythm within the design.

The landscape's patterns apply not only to plants but also to construction materials. For instance, use the same paving in one part of the backyard as in another to continue the pattern and flow. Use the same type of wood for decks, steps, and trellises; and look for existing patterns in your home's trim that you can echo in the landscape materials.

Rhythm is the sense of how your eye moves from one element to the next. This flow is created by repetition and contrast of size, form, line, color, and pattern. A sense of rhythm evolves from repeating

these elements and from using groups of the same plants throughout a design. Visual rhythm occurs when a planting gradually changes from large to small plants, from coarse textured to fine textured, or from groups of five, to groups of three, to a single specimen. Line and form also carry the eye in a definite direction or rhythm. Instead of using exact repetition, which may be monotonous, you can modify a rhythm — for example, by using pink and red instead of repeating just red.

Getting in on the Balancing Act

Balance is the sense of visual stability in a garden. Landscape designers usually attain balance by carefully placing plants and structures according to their size, color, and texture to equalize their visual weight or mass. Balance may be actual or perceived, which is why a landscape doesn't have to be perfectly symmetrical to be in balance. One side of a design may have plenty of heaviness due to large forms, strong colors, or rough textures, but it can be balanced by another area planted with a larger volume of smaller, lighter-colored, or more delicate-textured plants.

You can balance a large tree on one side of the backyard by placing a grouping of shrubs on the other side. A garden structure, such as a gazebo, on one side of the garden can be balanced by a tree on the other side. Drawing imaginary lines through the center of some of the landscape designs shown in the later chapters may help you understand how well balanced they are. You'll see that the placement of balancing features doesn't have to be exact, but the visual impact from the weight of the design on each side should be approximately equal.

16

Considering Scale and Proportion

Scale and proportion refer to the rightness of the size relationship between the various aspects of the landscape design and its site. For example, rarely is it advisable to use plants that will surely outgrow a small garden. Their size will be overwhelming—out of scale—from both practical and aesthetic points of view once they're mature.

Large-scale, tall, towering trees are in scale with a three-story house. Likewise, a confined walled garden space needs low or small-scale plants to be in scale with the planting space. A tiny island of ground covers planted in a ring beneath a tree makes the tree look top-heavy, because the ground-cover planting and the tree canopy are out of proportion. That's why the professional designs in this book employ large areas of ground cover to balance the scale of the trees and shrubs in the design.

SELECTING THE RIGHT PLANTS FOR YOUR BACKYARD LANDSCAPE

Plants perform a variety of functions in your backyard landscape. As previously mentioned, they constitute the garden's floor, walls, and ceiling. Besides being beautiful, plants provide privacy and shade; they can reduce noise, slow wind, control erosion, and supply food for your family as well as for birds, chipmunks, and other wildlife.

Don't neglect the regional adaptation and cultural requirements of plants when you landscape your yard. Some plants need cold winters, others freeze if the thermometer drops below 32°F; some thrive in intense heat, others wither in hot sun. Water-loving plants perform poorly in dry regions, and the same is true of desert plants in wet areas. No matter where you live, plants that are well adapted to the local climate will perform best and need the least care. That's why each landscape plan pictured in this book is available with plant lists tailored for eight different climatic regions of the United States and Canada. (See page 154 to order landscape blueprints.)

Choosing and Using Landscape Trees

Trees make up the tallest elements in most landscapes. They provide a framework for your backyard setting and give the landscape design visual strength. Tall deciduous shade trees, such as oak, maple, and sweetgum, contribute line, pattern, and form. They cast cooling shade in summer when they're fully leafed out, and they allow warming sun to reach your house and garden in winter when they're leafless.

Tree trunks provide strong vertical lines in the garden, while their branches create an overhead canopy of horizontal or curving lines. Their forms are primarily rounded, pyramidal, or weeping. Designers plant shade trees singly as specimens for a formal look, or group them for a woodsy or informal appearance. Because tree foliage reflects light and is studded with shadows, it contributes pattern and texture to a garden.

Ornamental flowering trees, such as crab apple, magnolia, and dogwood, are smaller than shade trees, which usually don't have much of a floral show. Although flowering trees can cast some needed shade on a patio, they're grown primarily for their bloom. These trees contribute color, line, pattern, and form to a design from their flowers, foliage, and fruit. When these smaller, ornamental trees are used alone, they draw the eye, creating a colorful focal point; when repeated, they contribute to the pattern and rhythm of the design.

A well-thought-out landscape plan locates shade trees far enough from the house so their limbs won't eventually grow onto the roof or cause damage if they break off in a storm. A good rule of thumb is to locate the trunk at least 20 feet from the house, but of course that depends on the ultimate height and width of the particular tree.

Deciduous shade trees planted 20 feet from the house on the south or west side will shade the house during the summer, lowering the indoor temperature by 8 to 20 degrees. In winter, when the tree is leafless, sunlight will warm the house, reducing heating costs.

Flowering or ornamental trees are usually somewhat smaller than shade trees, so designers usually place them where they're most visible and readily enjoyed. A flowering tree shows itself off well in almost any area of the garden, but it looks best with a simple background that plays up the flowers and silhouettes the branches. Place small trees as specimens in a lawn area or in a mixed border along a fence or property line where they'll help provide privacy.

Choosing and Using Landscape Shrubs

Shrubs are the most versatile of all landscape plants. Evergreen shrubs serve as foundation plantings, mark boundaries, and provide year-round privacy when used as screens and hedges. Their dependable greenery provides a beautiful background for the changing show of flowering shrubs. Deciduous flowering shrubs offer floral color, usually in spring or early summer, and many contribute brilliant fall color from leaves or berries. Because deciduous shrubs lose their foliage in winter, they become see-through and have much less visual weight during their leafless months than they have in summer.

When choosing shrubs, consider how their form, the texture of their leaves, and the pattern of their branches work in the overall landscape design. Choose shrubs whose mature size won't be out of scale with the landscape. Although you can keep shrubs small with proper pruning, this adds greatly to your gardening chores. And, all too often, when pruning controls a shrub's size, the plant gets trimmed into an unattractive — and unnatural — geometric shape.

You can save yourself a lot of work by planting and spacing shrubs according to their ultimate size, as is done in the professionally designed plans in this book. Check garden reference books for the mature sizes of any plants you're considering and avoid plants that, within several years, will block windows, crowd driveways and walks, or obscure a desirable view.

In most backyards, shrub borders create a wall along a property line or a background for a flower garden. They can also be used to separate different areas of the yard or to hide a security fence. A shrub border can consist of mixed plants — evergreen, deciduous, or both — or a single variety, but it looks most attractive when at least several plants of a particular type of shrub are planted together. When the border repeats masses of the same texture, form, line, or color, the planting looks intensified and visually more pleasing. Shrubs used as a background for a flower garden work best when planted with a single kind of plant, so the border doesn't detract from the flowers.

Use closely spaced tall shrubs and trees planted in a row to form hedges and screens. You can shear the hedge plants regularly to create a flat-walled hedge for a formal, tidy look, although you should realize that by doing so you're creating additional maintenance work for yourself. In most backyards, a row of

A shrub border of azaleas nestled in the shade beneath tall trees provides both privacy and bright spring flowers.

unpruned shrubs — chosen for their appropriate dimensions and left to grow into their natural arching or rounded shapes — is more fitting. Informal hedges definitely require less work.

A tall hedge or windbreak protecting your home can also conserve energy by slowing the wind. An evergreen windbreak blocking the prevailing wind, which usually comes from the north or west side of a property, can cut winter heating costs in some cold climates by as much as 30 percent. It also creates more comfortable conditions for sitting outdoors on a patio or deck.

When using a tall hedge or evergreen trees as a windbreak, plant individual plants in a staggered row rather than a straight row. Wind flows up and over a straight row of plants, whereas a staggered row changes the course of the air for a longer distance. Generally, maximum wind reduction occurs at a distance equal to four to six times the height of the hedge, so plantings should be established at that distance from the house. For example, plant an 8-foot-high hedge 32 to 48 feet from the house.

Go for Ground Cover Plants

Low-growing plants that blanket the soil are called ground covers. These plants work well in low-traffic areas and in parts of the garden where a high-maintenance lawn is undesirable or would be difficult to mow but where an open feeling is needed. Ground covers used on slopes help prevent soil erosion, as well as make the area easier to maintain. Beds of ground covers beneath shrubs unify the planting design and set off the shrubbery while improving the soil and shading out most weeds.

Many kinds of plants serve admirably as ground covers, although evergreen types that spread rapidly look best and cost the least for covering large areas. Among the most widely used, vinca, pachysandra, and ajuga produce attractive flowers as well as beautiful foliage.

Speaking Up for Climbing Vines

Vines make excellent landscape plants for screening small areas and covering fences, arbors, and trellises with greenery and flowers. They can soften stark fences, corners, and rough walls, and they're especially useful in narrow spaces where ground space is at a premium. Many homeowners allow vines to climb up the side of the house to great effect. However, the clinging roots and tendrils of some vines can damage mortar and loosen clapboards. A better choice is to grow a vine on a trellis placed several inches from the surface of the house.

Vines growing on a house wall or on a trellis placed next to the wall will block the sun's heat in summer and insulate against the cold in winter. Place deciduous vines on south and west walls to block summer heat and allow winter warmth to come through. Use evergreen vines on a north wall, where they'll provide insulation.

The Charm of Flowers

Garden flowers — bulbs, annuals, and perennials — grow fast and beautify your yard with showy blossoms. Few other kinds of garden plants provide as much pleasure as quickly. In most regions, many kinds of bulbs, annuals, and perennials decorate backyards with their profuse blossoms.

Bulbs and perennials grow and bloom for several weeks during their special season of the year. The foliage of most perennials endures for the entire growing season and then dies back to the ground for winter, while most spring-flowering bulbs go dormant by mid-summer. Perennials and hardy bulbs come back the next spring, regrowing from dormant roots. Annuals live for only one growing season and then die, although some types reseed themselves. The allure of annuals is that, as long as faded blossoms are plucked off, the plants will bloom for months on end — usually right up until frost.

Whether you choose spring-flowering bulbs for their early-season color, annuals for their continual bright summer color, or perennials for their dependable performance, you'll get the most landscape impact if you plant in large drifts of a single variety, as the designs in this book illustrate.

Many of the designs feature masses of bulbs and lovely, long-blooming, easy-care perennials for a colorful summer display. The bulbs and perennials are planted directly in a swathe of evergreen ground cover. A mass planting of a single color in a backyard garden creates a greater impact, especially when viewed from a distant window or patio, than a smaller grouping or a grouping of many different flowers. Another part of the beauty of this arrangement is that the ground cover remains the year around to dress up the garden even when the bulbs or perennials are out of bloom or have gone dormant.

Bulbs, perennials, and ground covers will grow happily together as long as their sizes and cultural needs are matched. For instance, daffodils that reach 10 to 12 inches high work well with a ground cover of pachysandra 4 to 6 inches high.

If you're an avid flower gardener, however, you'll want a more intricate garden to indulge your hobby. Designs for specialty perennial gardens featuring an assortment of beautiful flowers are included in Chapter 10. You can add any of these to most existing backyards, or design a landscape to include one of these gardens along the lot line or as an island bed. Professionally designed landscapes, such as those presented in this book, enhance a home's beauty while adding to its value. Study the designs on the following pages — they're divided into themed chapters to suit your family's needs — to see how to achieve professional results without hiring a professional.

Landscape design: Ireland-Gannon Associates

A vine-covered arbor and bench welcome visitors into the backyard and provide a shady spot to sit.

Spring-blooming narcissus make a great splash of color when planted in a large mass. The hostas will grow larger and as summer arrives their green-and-white leaves will mask the yellowing foliage of the dormant bulbs.

19

This charming Victorian playhouse will look great in any backyard. The house sleeps eight children and its yard features two swings hanging from an arbor. The plans are available for do-it-yourselfers; see page 151.

BACKYARDS FOR CHILDREN

Your Whole Family Will Delight in These Yards Designed for Creative Games and Active Play

Turn loose a couple of five-year-old boys or girls on an acre of land containing a lawn, an old tree, a stand of tall grass, a pile of scrap lumber, and a regulation jungle gym, and where do you think you'll find the kids playing? Anywhere but on the jungle gym. Kids are inventive and easily bored and they'll take over any available space, whether you've gone to great lengths to plan for them or not.

It takes more than a swing set to keep children occupied for any extended period of time. Set aside a corner of a 60-foot lot, label it for children only, and the very best you'll be able to say is that you've acknowledged your kids' right to have their own play space. If you're wise you'll realize that your children will use not just the sandbox, swing set, and basketball hoop but the entire yard as a playground, and you'll design the yard accordingly. The four plans in this chapter are great examples of yards where both children and parents will be at home.

DETERMINING YOUR FAMILY'S NEEDS

The first step in designing a yard for children is to take time to think about your kids' particular styles of play. What are their favorite toys, games, and activities? Are your children physically active types

who are likely to need lots of space to run, jump, and ride, or are they more contemplative and happy to play in one spot for hours? Do they pay attention to boundaries, or do they often forget what they're doing in the excitement of play? Make a list of your overall backyard requirements and then consider how you can accomplish them in your particular site. (You'll find specific advice about this step in Chapter 1, "Landscape Your Backyard the Professional Way," beginning on page 6.)

Don't neglect to ask your children what they would like in a play yard. They'll be pleased to be involved in the process, and you may make some important discoveries. Perhaps they're more interested in having a place to dig than a place to swing. Maybe one child dreams of having a playhouse or a tree house, whereas the other would love a hopscotch court. Or perhaps one child prefers to have space to make a personal garden, whereas another is happy to assist you in your garden.

Your backyard design doesn't have to be complicated to succeed for both you and your children. Focus on the basic elements of your landscape—the placement of the patio, lawn, trees, shrubs, and special play equipment. You can always elaborate the details later. Children are easy to please, so you

Children learn responsibility by caring for their own garden — with a little help from you — and delight in watching the plants grow and change.

needn't invest in an expensive playhouse or other structure if the cost is beyond your budget. A hiding place, even if it's carved out of a shrubbery border, can be a special place for a child. It needn't be completely enclosed. An overhanging branch, an old tree stump, or a low wall can provide enough camouflage or protection to become the basis for an imaginary fort or playhouse. A sturdy, low-branched tree can be a great resource for a child. Besides providing an exciting place for climbing, the tree can serve as a support for a swing, rope ladder, or tree house.

When you're figuring out your family's requirements, keep the following in mind.

- Children have wonderful imaginations. Encourage them by providing interesting nooks and crannies for hiding places. Create trails through the shrubbery and yard for exploring and make-believe games.
- Kids love to climb. If you don't have a good climbing tree in your yard, consider providing some type of structure for that purpose. Otherwise, they'll find something less safe.
- Children need both hard and soft surfaces to play on. A lawn is an ideal place for tumbling and roughhousing; paving works better for bike riding and basketball.
- Children like to have something of their very own. To get kids interested in gardening and science, give them a small garden spot of their own and help them grow the fruits and vegetables they like to eat.
- Kids play exuberantly. Design your landscape with tough plants, and protect your own garden space from balls and bike wheels with fencing or hedges.
- Children grow up before you know it. Plan ahead for when the kids are older and won't need a yard for active playing. Locate the sandbox where it can be easily transformed into an attractive raised strawberry bed, or construct the kid's vegetable garden where a cut-flower bed would be perfect.
- Youngsters need supervision. Design a children's yard so that all play areas can be seen from indoors and from the patio or terrace. Fences with locked gates provide additional security.

PLANNING FOR SAFE PLAY

Children love to play outdoors and the fresh air invigorates them—and you. When your children are young, you'll have to pay more attention to designing a play space that won't cause skinned knees and is resistant to the wear and tear of active feet. Once they're older and more independent, your kids may become interested in group sports and you can remake the yard, adding a badminton court or a hard-surfaced shuffleboard court where the entire family can play together.

Soft and Green

The ultimate paving for active children is grass, and a patch of lawn is often first on a parent's backyard landscaping list. No other surface feels as soft and cool underfoot or looks as attractive. A lawn doesn't need to be large to be useful. In small backyards, and in areas where water is in short supply, 600 to 800 square feet is more than enough to provide a soft, resilient surface for your kids to play on. Adding a berm, or raised area, to an otherwise flat lawn provides a fun place for kids to turn somersaults and build fortresses.

When choosing a lawn grass, be sure to select one suited to the requirements of your site. Mixes of several varieties are available for sunny, shady, or dry situations. You may also wish to choose a mixture of especially durable grasses to resist the wear and tear of active play and sports.

The Advantages of a Hard Surface

For riding bikes, pulling wagons, or playing hopscotch, hard paving is essential. If, for safety reasons, you don't like your kids playing in the street or driveway, provide a paved surface, such as concrete, brick, stone, or wood, in the backyard for such activities. Pea gravel, decomposed granite, and sand are other good options. Poured concrete, the best surface for wheeled toys, can be finished in different textures to make it more attractive. You'll find concrete and stone pavers in a variety of shapes and colors. Try to select a material and color that works well with your house and surroundings.

The Pleasures of Sand

The tactile pleasure of sand never quite leaves us, and children glory in it. A sandbox provides a source of entertainment for toddlers and grade-school youngsters. Easily added to any backyard, a sandbox can be as simple as a rubber tire or an inflated play pool filled with sharp builder's sand. (Avoid beach sand, which is too salty and can affect the pH of your soil.) A large sandbox located beneath a play structure provides a great place for digging and building, while taking the injury out of falls and jumps. You can build a traditional sandbox from wood siding or construct a raised bed and fill it with sand. Cover the box and it becomes a seat. When your children grow older, you can turn the sandbox into a planter.

If the patio paving covers a wide area and includes some kind of geometric pattern, try filling a section or two with sand to make a ground-level sandbox near an area where adults will lounge. The paving will prevent the sand from spreading too far. When the children outgrow the sandbox, you can repave the area or plant it with flowers or ground covers.

To keep the sand from getting muddy, it's a good idea to separate it from the soil beneath with landscape fabric. A cover for the sandbox—made from a plastic sheet, canvas, wood, or acrylic—will keep rain, pets, and debris out.

ENTICING PLAY STRUCTURES

All kinds of play structures—from the standard metal swing set to elaborate wood structures that include swings, turrets, and monkey bars—are available ready-made. The big advantage of a prefabricated structure is that the engineering has already been done to ensure its sturdiness and safety. But you can make a simple swing with nothing more than a strong rope with a knot at the end and a board for the seat. A tree house can consist of a sturdy platform with a ladder and a railing.

When attaching a swing or other structure to a tree, use ropes rather than nails to secure it. Nails may damage the tree and perhaps shorten its life. Check the ropes at frequent intervals to make sure they remain safe and strong.

If you decide to build a structure, be sure to use rot-resistant timber, such as cedar or redwood, or choose pressure-treated wood. Recognize, however, that even rot-resistant redwood lasts only five or six years if it's in direct contact with the soil, so use pressure-treated lumber in such places. For safety's sake, it's always better to overbuild and to use bolts instead of nails. Be sure to place the structure where the children can be easily seen by a supervising adult.

A GARDEN SPOT ALL THEIR OWN

You can help children learn about gardening and nature by providing them with a space all their own to plant vegetable and flower seeds. Choose plants that germinate easily and grow quickly, such as radishes, or plants that produce interesting fruit, such as gourds or luffas.

If you have the room, you and your children will be rewarded by planting a tree together—perhaps to commemorate someone's birthday or a special holiday. Children understand that they're growing, and they're eager to watch and compare other growing things. If your site is moist, try a weeping willow. In drier areas, poplars, alders, and eucalyptus grow fast despite the conditions. Slower but more long-lived trees, such as oaks, make good landscape choices.

This chapter presents four backyard plans that were developed for families with active children. Study each design to see how suitable the yard is for your children's play styles, how well the landscape fits your particular site, and how easily it can be adapted to meet your family's changing interests and needs.

Children's Play Yard

If there's one thing that can be said about children's play areas, it's that their function usually far outweighs their attractiveness. However, this backyard design presents an excellent solution to a functional children's play yard that is still pleasing to look at. The backyard includes all the fun elements a child would love. On one side of the yard are grouped a play structure for climbing and swinging, a playhouse, and a sandbox enclosed in a low boardwalk. A play mound—a perfect place for running, leaping, and holding fort — rises from the lawn on the other side of the yard.

These play areas are integrated into the landscape by their circular form, which is repeated in the sandbox, play mound, boardwalk, and the sand areas under the playhouse and play structure. The curved brick patio and planting border carry though the circular theme. The stepping stones leading to the play areas also follow a circular path — a playful pattern that invites a child to "follow the yellow brick road."

From the house and patio, the views of both the garden and the play areas are unobstructed, affording constant adult supervision from both indoors and out. The border surrounding the yard creates a private setting that offers a changing show of flowers from the masses of shrubs and perennials. Beyond the play structure, a large tree shades the area, providing landscape interest, and perhaps even a place for adventurous young feet to climb.

When the children are grown, this design can be adapted as a playground for older folk by removing the playhouse and play structure and planting lawn, or a flower or vegetable garden.

Regionalized Plant Lists

Because climate and growing conditions vary greatly throughout North America, it is impossible to list here all the plants for this landscape plan that would do well everywhere on the continent. However, you can order a Blueprint Package with plant lists keyed to this plan and selected by expert horticulturists to thrive in your area.

The six-page Blueprint Package features a large-size version of this Plan View, plus a detailed regional Plant and Materials List. It also includes an illustrated list of hundreds of landscape plants suited to your region, in case you wish to make substitutions, as well as planting instructions and plant adaptation maps to ensure professional results with your new landscape.

See page 157 to order your regionalized Blueprint Package.

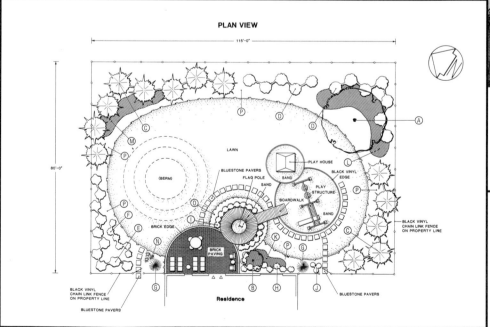

Landscape Plan L244 shown in summer
Designed by Michael J. Opisso

Here is a special backyard designed for both children and adults. The yard offers youngsters their own place to escape into a world of imagination and discovery without compromising the attractiveness of a garden setting.

A child can skip right along the stepping-stones to tend a personal vegetable garden in this cleverly designed backyard. With a barn-and-silo playhouse and compost bin adjacent to the garden, your child can exercise imagination in creative play while helping with the chores and learning about recycling. For more vigorous games, the swing set surrounded by a timber-edged sand pit will help the youngster soar.

Kid's Vegetable Garden in the Round

Young gardeners will thrive in this backyard, which is specially designed to entice a child into horticulture with a circular vegetable garden and a barn-and-silo playhouse or toolshed. The stepping-stones in the garden make a perfect spot for hopscotch, and the swing set, sandbox, and lawn provide other places to romp.

Vegetables grow just as well in beds as in rows, and the circular bed used here better suits a child's sense of necessary disorder. Surrounded by a gravel path and crisscrossed by pathways, the garden presents four individual easy-care beds that can be planted with several types of vegetables. Begin with your child's favorites in order to create enthusiasm for gardening. Then add a few new ones to encourage investigation. Eating a vine-ripened tomato grown personally by the child may be enough to convert a typical play-obsessed ten-year-old into a life-long gardener.

Parents will like this backyard design, too. It combines a permanent structure of easy-care trees, shrubs, and perennials, which produce a beautiful color display spring through fall, and a handsome brick patio for relaxing and entertaining. The circular shape of the vegetable bed, which can be turned into a pretty herb or flower bed if the kids lose interest, echoes the curves of the lawn, making it an attractive, yet functional, design element. For safety's sake, the entire backyard is open and visible from the patio and has only one gate.

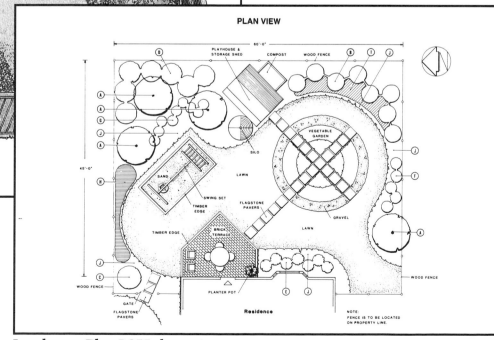

PLAN VIEW

Landscape Plan L255 shown in summer
Designed by Michael J. Opisso

For prefabricated storage shed, see page 150.

Regionalized Plant Lists

Because climate and growing conditions vary greatly throughout North America, it is impossible to list here all the plants for this landscape plan that would do well everywhere on the continent. However, you can order a Blueprint Package with plant lists keyed to this plan and selected by expert horticulturists to thrive in your area.

The six-page Blueprint Package features a large-size version of this Plan View, plus a detailed regional Plant and Materials List. It also includes an illustrated list of hundreds of landscape plants suited to your region, in case you wish to make substitutions, as well as planting instructions and plant adaptation maps to ensure professional results with your new landscape.

See page 157 to order your regionalized Blueprint Package.

27

The ideal backyard for a sports-minded family, this
design features three permanent playing fields to
provide children and adults with plenty of play options. The parklike arrangement of trees gives the
yard generous shade and screening, while the border
of evergreen shrubs establishes privacy and muffles
enthusiastic cheers.

Backyard Play Courts for Action Games

If your family is the energetic kind that never stops moving, this backyard plan provides the perfect solution for soaking up all their enthusiasm. Three play courts are permanently installed: shuffleboard, badminton, and hopscotch. All are discreetly integrated with other elements of the landscape to create a beautiful, but functional, backyard.

In the center of the lawn, the outer dimensions of a volleyball or badminton court are marked inconspicuously with landscape timbers laid on edge flush with the ground. Set this way, they don't interfere with mowing or cause anyone to trip, yet they remain as clear markers. You can make bolder, but temporary, official court lines in the lawn with garden lime, gypsum, or flour—none of which will harm the grass.

The shuffleboard and hopscotch courts in the perimeter of the yard are made from poured concrete. Both are partially hidden behind shrubs and trees and are surrounded by an evergreen ground cover to soften their hard edges. Younger children will delight in the circular timber-edged sandbox, which can be turned into a flower or strawberry bed when the kids outgrow sand-castle and fort building.

The brick patio, attractively curved to mimic the shape of the lawn, allows plenty of space for adults to relax in the sun, dine outdoors, and enjoy a commanding view of all the sports action.

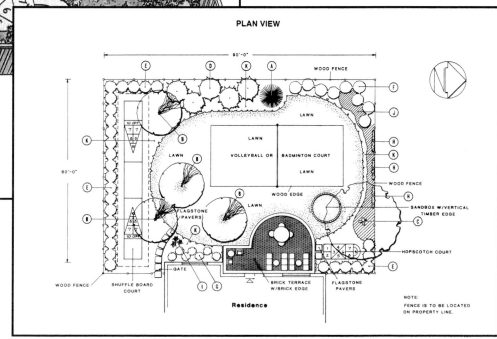

PLAN VIEW

Landscape Plan L256 shown in summer
Designed by Michael J. Opisso

Regionalized Plant Lists

Because climate and growing conditions vary greatly throughout North America, it is impossible to list here all the plants for this landscape plan that would do well everywhere on the continent. However, you can order a Blueprint Package with plant lists keyed to this plan and selected by expert horticulturists to thrive in your area.

The six-page Blueprint Package features a large-size version of this Plan View, plus a detailed regional Plant and Materials List. It also includes an illustrated list of hundreds of landscape plants suited to your region, in case you wish to make substitutions, as well as planting instructions and plant adaptation maps to ensure professional results with your new landscape.

See page 157 to order your regionalized Blueprint Package.

Play Yard for Budding Gymnasts

Your young, active children—and their friends—will enjoy hours of engaging play in this wonderful backyard. The elaborate play structures, which are designed to exercise every growing muscle a kid has to develop, feature many different elements—a hanging tire, pull-up bars, slides, swings, and rings, as well as platforms for game playing. With so many choices, a child's short attention span is sure to be accommodated. Besides the obvious play structures, the yard includes secret hiding places nestled behind the shrubs and under the trees in the yard's corners—these will lure any child in need of a quiet, contemplative moment.

The repeating circles beneath the play structures create the landscape's main design feature. These are actually giant sand pits that minimize the possibility of your budding gymnasts injuring themselves from falls. They're bordered by easy-to-install vinyl strips that keep the sand from spilling onto the lawn. With the play structures set off center of the yard, plenty of lawn area remains for running games and visual beauty.

Although a wood fence at the property line borders the yard for security reasons, the densely planted trees and shrubs enhance the sense of privacy and enclosure, while providing colorful flowers and softening greenery. The wood deck, accessible from the house through sliding glass doors, balances the visual weight of the play structure. The deck's diagonal lines and squared-off shape make a happy contrast with the circular sand pits.

Regionalized Plant Lists

Because climate and growing conditions vary greatly throughout North America, it is impossible to list here all the plants for this landscape plan that would do well everywhere on the continent. However, you can order a Blueprint Package with plant lists keyed to this plan and selected by expert horticulturists to thrive in your area.

The six-page Blueprint Package features a large-size version of this Plan View, plus a detailed regional Plant and Materials List. It also includes an illustrated list of hundreds of landscape plants suited to your region, in case you wish to make substitutions, as well as planting instructions and plant adaptation maps to ensure professional results with your new landscape.

See page 157 to order your regionalized Blueprint Package.

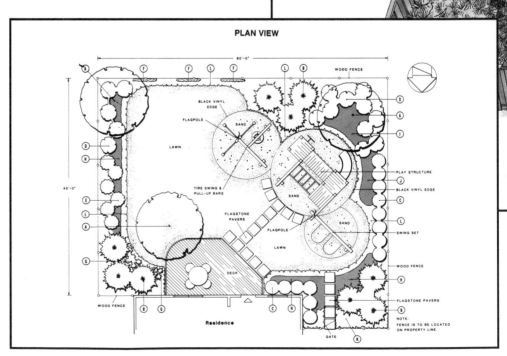

PLAN VIEW

Landscape Plan L257 shown in spring
Designed by Damon Scott
For Deck Plan D115, see page 152.

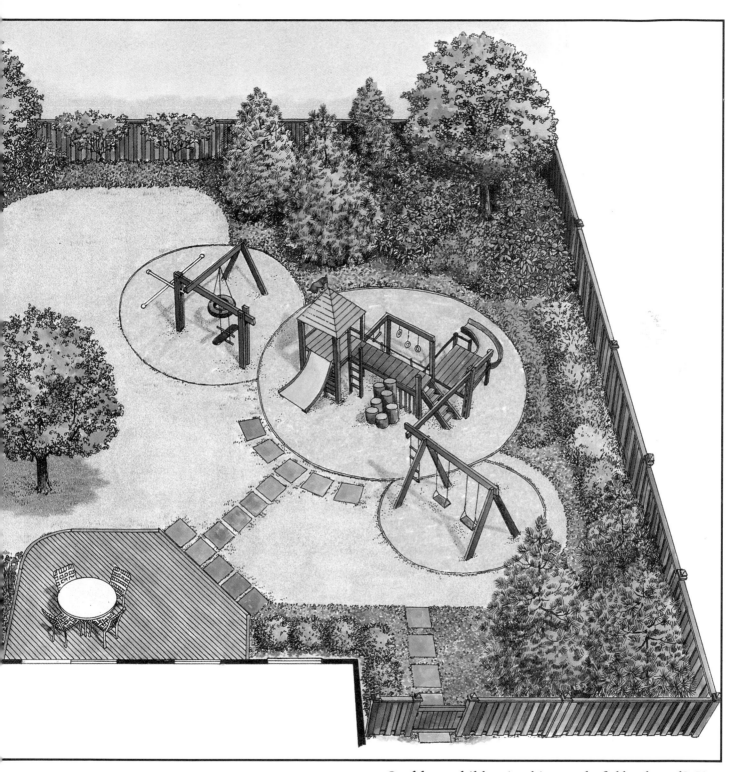

Could any child resist this wonderful backyard? Circular sand pits — designed for both play and safety — combined with a fabulous play structure makes this backyard as exciting as the local park. Mom and Dad will enjoy the yard's parklike beauty as much as the kids enjoy its playground allure.

Landscape design: Conni Cross

Simulating a rugged outcropping on an alpine slope, this rock garden offers a unique gardening opportunity for avid gardeners to grow unusual plants.

LANDSCAPING NATURE'S WAY

Bring Wildflowers and the Natural Look Into Your Own Backyard

Naturalistic landscapes—the kind that mimic the beauty of the forests, fields, mountains, or deserts—are in vogue these days because, when properly executed, they're ecologically and environmentally sound and refreshing to look at. Because this design style mimics Nature's wild, untamed appearance and relies on native or well-adapted plants, such landscapes usually require less maintenance and less water than traditional gardens—which translates into less drain on our natural resources.

Naturalistic landscapes encompass an informal, it-just-happened look, perhaps even appearing as if Nature herself positioned the plants. But, like any other style of landscape design, successful naturalistic designs don't happen without careful thought and planning. Although casual in mood, naturalistic designs still need to bow to the rules of form, texture, and color, and to incorporate all the plants and elements of the landscape into a visually pleasing, well-balanced design. While working to achieve a naturalistic look, the designer strives to create an attractive setting that meets the family's needs for outdoor living space.

The plans included in this chapter are suited to a variety of site conditions. A large, open, sunny lot with unimproved soil can be transformed into a beautiful flowering meadow reflecting the beauty of the open countryside, or into a rocky garden reminiscent of a rugged mountain setting. If your yard has tall shade trees, consider them an asset and elaborate upon the cool shade by planting a woodland wildflower garden instead of cursing the lawn grass that struggles to grow in the poor light. If the sound of a babbling brook or the quiet reflections mirrored on a still lake captivate you, bring them home by installing a garden pool near the outdoor sitting area—then you won't have to leave home to enjoy the peace that Nature offers.

THINKING NATURALISTICALLY

Take a good look at your property and consider the growing conditions you discover. Respect the conditions you meet—such as poor rocky soil, wet boggy soil, or deep shade—and devise a plan and planting scheme that adapts to that habitat rather than fights it. Keep in mind that much is gained by what you avoid doing! Respect what is there, and don't try to make your yard into something it can't be without inordinate effort or drastic change.

Observing the natural landscape where you live can provide design inspiration. Notice the types of trees and shrubs that appeal to you, their colors, how they are grouped, and how they are spaced in their natural state. Notice the color of the soil and the rocks. These are the primary cues to use when you landscape naturally.

Although it may be admirable to try to re-create the natural landscape that once existed in your community, don't worry if inspiration comes from afar: You may wish to mimic a forest scene you enjoyed while hiking in the Smoky Mountains by planting native wildflowers and ferns beneath the tree boughs, or perhaps re-create a meadow scene you enjoyed during a vacation in New England. As

plant palette by incorporating species from different, but climatically similar, regions. For instance, you could plant field flowers native to Europe, such as Flanders poppies, along with the prairie wildflowers used in the Backyard Meadow Garden (see Plan L258 on page 36).

Choosing plants that fit the style and growing conditions of the garden and arranging them as if they were planted by the wind is the key to using plants well in a naturalistic design. Avoid shrubs pruned into artificial balls and cubes, and allow

Favorite plants for the "new American garden," ornamental grass and hybrid black-eyed-Susans mimic the beauty of the great American prairie in a combination that's showy for months.

long as the plan and the plants you choose find the growing conditions on your property compatible, your garden will look as if Nature herself did it.

Plant Choices — Going Native

Many people have a misconception about native plants. They think that native means disease resistant, drought tolerant, and low maintenance. The truth is far from this notion. Native plants may be all of these things—but, just like garden varieties, they can suffer unless they receive the growing conditions they need. Plant a drought-tolerant native shrub in dry soil and it will do just fine; plant it in a bog and it will drown. Native plants can and do flourish in gardens where they're properly situated because they're adapted to the local climate and conditions, but they get their share of bugs just like other plants.

Although you may wish to rely on wildflowers and native plants in your naturalistic garden, you needn't shun exotics—those plants from other parts of the country or the world. You can extend your

plants to cascade and spread according to their own innate grace. Casually tuck plants in and around each other or allow them to peek out from under rocks, rather than planting them in rigid rows.

MAKING A BACKYARD MEADOW

A summer drive in the country may reveal an enchanting scenery of open, sunny fields filled with waving grasses and studded with bright wildflowers. Unlike a woodland, which has an inward meditative feeling, a meadow garden is a place of sweeping vistas. If you have an open, sunny property, you can re-create this bucolic scene—and create a low-maintenance landscape to boot—by planting a backyard meadow garden.

Once established, a meadow garden requires little maintenance, usually only an annual mowing. A meadow may be the perfect solution for quickly and economically landscaping a barren piece of property, especially around a newly built house on former farmland, or a large property with too much high-maintenance lawn.

Meadow gardening became a fad during the last decade; however, misconceptions abound about how to get started. It's not as simple as ceasing to mow the lawn and scattering a can of wildflower seeds. Most lawn grasses are the wrong kind of grass for a meadow, since they form competitive runners rather than grow in the well-behaved bunches that allow wildflowers to get started. A backyard meadow needs careful soil preparation, installation, watering, and weeding to get established. First, till the soil and remove all existing weeds; allow weed seedlings to germinate and till them under or apply glyphosate, a quick-degrading herbicide. You can sow the seeds two weeks after the herbicide treatment.

Since many wildflower seed mixes fail to germinate or their flowers don't reseed and return during the following years, the Backyard Meadow Garden (see Plan L258 on page 36) relies on a different, surefire meadow-gardening method. By planting container-grown perennials—natives adapted to prairies and meadows—rather than wildflower seeds, and then sowing native bunchgrass seeds around the flowers, you'll be assured of instant and long-lasting results that won't disappoint you. Keep the new meadow well watered and pull weeds regularly during the first year—and your meadow will be here to stay. You must mow the meadow every year in late fall or winter to eliminate woody invaders whose seeds inevitably crop up in the meadow. Without mowing, the meadow is likely to revert to a bramble patch and then to a forest. You can also create paths with your mower during the growing season to provide both views and access.

WOODLAND WILDFLOWER AND SHADE GARDENS

A yard with large shade trees can be transformed into a beautiful woodland or shade garden by incorporating tiers of shade-loving plants. Arrange the plants by height to attain a layering of foliage from the ground to the sky. For example, plant ground covers in drifts or islands to carpet the garden with foliage. Then, to draw the eye upward, plant medium-sized to large shrubs. Use understory trees to spread a flowery and leafy canopy just above eye level.

The Shade Garden (see Plan L242 on page 38) features an informal, naturalistic look but uses readily available, shade-loving shrubs and flowers to create the feeling of a natural woodland. The Woodland Wildflower Walk (see Plan L260 on page 45) features a collector's dream of native wildflowers and a pond to capture the realistic mood of a stroll in the woods.

If your wooded property is overgrown, you may need to remove brush to make more room for choice small trees and shrubs. Crowded trees may be selectively removed and the canopies of others thinned to shape the space and to enhance the natural forms of the remaining trees. Once the forest canopy is in order, you can design and plant the woodland floor.

Since most shade-loving plants require a soil rich in humus, you may need to add lots of organic matter to improve your soil. The acidity, structure, and moisture content of woodland soils should be protected with a thick mulch of wood chips, shredded leaves, or other organic matter, which will also nourish the plants and discourage weeds.

ROCKS AND BOULDERS FOR A CRAGGY LOOK

Slopes and steep grades provide obvious opportunities for creating a rock garden reminiscent of a mountaintop or desert landscape. Flat sites pose more challenge, but by contouring the land and adding even a small change in levels, as is done in Rugged and Rocky (see Plan L259 on page 40), you can incorporate some interesting craggy outcrops and sustain the naturalistic illusion by thoroughly screening the surrounding terrain with evergreen and deciduous trees.

When building a rock garden, use only one kind of rock for the most natural look. Sedimentary rock is the easiest to build with because its flat sides lend themselves to stacking into dry walls and ledges. Place large rocks and boulders in the landscape first—they're the backbone of the design. Then, smaller rocks and even patches of pea gravel can be fitted into the design. Rocks should be partially buried, not set on top of the ground.

WATER IN THE GARDEN

Whether still and reflecting or moving and image shattering, water can bring peace, energy, or coolness into the garden. An informal pond or waterfall edged with plants or river rock paving (see Plan L253 on page 42) can be made to look like a real pond, adding the final touch to a naturalistic landscape design.

Installing a pond is a weekend task for two do-it-yourselfers. Easily accomplished with a vinyl liner or a prefabricated fiberglass shell, a pond can also be constructed of concrete. Goldfish and water plants keep the pool ecologically balanced and any mosquitoes under control. A good reference book for do-it-yourself pond builders is *Garden Pools and Fountains* published by Ortho Books.

Study the plans on the following pages to get a feel for the restfulness offered by naturalistic designs. Choose the one that best fits where you live, how you live, and the site conditions offered by your backyard. Whether you want a meadow or woodland garden, a rock or water garden, you'll find the ideas and inspiration here to create a natural oasis in your own backyard.

This plan re-creates one of Nature's great spectacles: a grassy meadow brimming with blooming flowers. A deck of wood planking rises above the level of the yard so you can appreciate the view from on high. Steps lead down to naturalistic stone paving that feathers into lawn. Once established, this meadow garden will prove to be easy to maintain, easy on the eye, and easy on the environment.

Backyard Meadow Garden

If you yearn for the look and feel of a flower-drenched meadow, this low-maintenance landscape plan can help you create it in your very own backyard. The small lawn needs normal mowing maintenance, but, once established, the wildflower meadow requires only once-a-year mowing to a height of 6 inches in late fall or winter to keep it blooming and to prevent woody plants from invading.

The designer created the wildflower meadow using a field grass and sun-loving perennial wildflowers—those at home on prairies and in open meadows. You'll be assured of success with this garden, because you start it from container-grown flowers planted together with meadow grass seeds. Unlike totally seeded meadow gardens, which are difficult at best to get established, this method ensures that the flowering plants become quickly rooted and spread year after year into a gorgeous spectacle of blossoms set against wavy green grass. You'll have to weed between plants the first season or two until the desirable flowers and grass become established enough to crowd out weeds.

A rustic, stacked-rail fence, in keeping with the bucolic theme of the garden, separates the manicured lawn from the meadow, taming its wildness just a bit. Plantings near the house include informal plants, such as ornamental grasses, that echo the wilder look of the plants in the meadow. Drought-tolerant evergreen trees, grouped strategically in the meadow, provide privacy and wind screening in addition to giving the yard permanent structure and year-round beauty.

Regionalized Plant Lists

Because climate and growing conditions vary greatly throughout North America, it is impossible to list here all the plants for this landscape plan that would do well everywhere on the continent. However, you can order a Blueprint Package with plant lists keyed to this plan and selected by expert horticulturists to thrive in your area.

The six-page Blueprint Package features a large-size version of this Plan View, plus a detailed regional Plant and Materials List. It also includes an illustrated list of hundreds of landscape plants suited to your region, in case you wish to make substitutions, as well as planting instructions and plant adaptation maps to ensure professional results with your new landscape.

See page 157 to order your regionalized Blueprint Package.

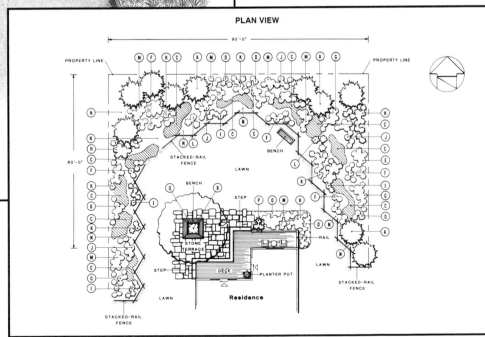

PLAN VIEW

Landscape Plan L258 shown in summer
Designed by Damon Scott

Shade Garden

Woe to the gardener who has to deal with established tall trees that cast a great deal of shade — a beautiful, colorful backyard is out of the question. Right? Wrong! Nothing could be further from the truth, as demonstrated by this artfully designed shade garden. The key to working with large existing trees is in using the shade as an asset, not as a liability, and in choosing shade-loving plants to grow beneath them. If the trees have a very dense canopy, branches can be selectively removed to thin the trees and create filtered shade below.

In this plan, the designer shapes the lawn and beds to respond to the locations of the trees. Note that all but one of the trees are situated in planting beds, not open lawn. Placing a single tree in the lawn helps to integrate the lawn and planting beds, creating a cohesive design. At the right, the deep planting area is enhanced by pavers, a bench, and a birdbath, creating an inviting shady retreat. Near the house, a small patio provides a lounging spot; its curving shape echoes the curving form of the planting beds.

Throughout the garden, perennials, woody plants, and ground covers are arranged in drifts to create a comfortable and serene space. The garden is in constant but ever-changing bloom from early spring through fall as its special plants—ones chosen because they thrive in just such a shady setting in their native habitats—go in and out of bloom. And fall brings big splashes of foliage color to complete the year-long show. To provide the finishing carpet to this beautiful and cool shade garden, choose a grass-seed variety selected to tolerate shade.

Regionalized Plant Lists

Because climate and growing conditions vary greatly throughout North America, it is impossible to list here all the plants for this landscape plan that would do well everywhere on the continent. However, you can order a Blueprint Package with plant lists keyed to this plan and selected by expert horticulturists to thrive in your area.

The six-page Blueprint Package features a large-size version of this Plan View, plus a detailed regional Plant and Materials List. It also includes an illustrated list of hundreds of landscape plants suited to your region, in case you wish to make substitutions, as well as planting instructions and plant adaptation maps to ensure professional results with your new landscape.

See page 157 to order your regionalized Blueprint Package.

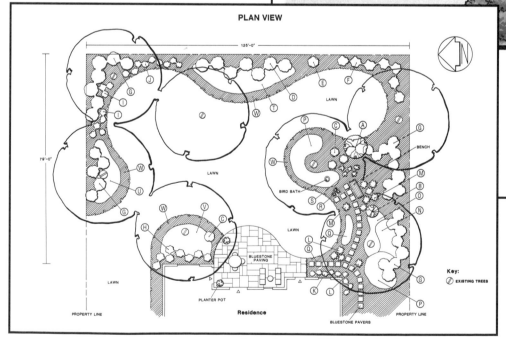

Landscape Plan L242 shown in spring
Designed by Michael J. Opisso

Shaded yards need not be dark and dull, as this backyard design demonstrates. Here, beneath the shadows of seven mature trees, a colorful collection of shade-loving shrubs, perennials, and ground covers flourishes.

Rugged and Rocky

Take your cue from Mother Nature: If you love the rocky out-croppings of the mountains or deserts, that may be the way to go in your garden. Boulders—single and sturdy, combined into groupings, or stacked for low walls—bring to a garden a solidity and substance that's impossible to create any other way. And rocky sites create an environment for a variety of special plants.

The designer raised the soil level of the yard slightly to create a curving contour at the back of the yard. The soil is retained by a wall of large boulders on one side and rough-chiseled natural stones forming a simple, low, curvilinear dry wall on the other side. Underneath the trees and between the rocks and boulders various creeping plants spread and spill their way toward the lawn. A combination of drought-tolerant deciduous and evergreen shrubs and trees provides softening foliage and flowers.

Flagstone pavers allow for circulation from the garden gates to the stone-paved terrace, which features two levels that are only a stair-step different in height. Several types of creeping, fragrant paving plants mingle between the stones, releasing their scent when walked on. Rock-garden plants mix in a chaos of color among the scattered boulders in the gravel-surfaced planting bed near the patio.

The permanent structure provided by the plants, large boulders, and paving stones creates a garden of year-round beauty. You can follow the designer's lead and grow the easy-care plants called for in the design. However, rock-garden devotees may wish to tuck in their own collections of rare and exotic alpine plants, which will happily meld into this stunning naturalistic design.

Regionalized Plant Lists

Because climate and growing conditions vary greatly throughout North America, it is impossible to list here all the plants for this landscape plan that would do well everywhere on the continent. However, you can order a Blueprint Package with plant lists keyed to this plan and selected by expert horticulturists to thrive in your area.

The six-page Blueprint Package features a large-size version of this Plan View, plus a detailed regional Plant and Materials List. It also includes an illustrated list of hundreds of landscape plants suited to your region, in case you wish to make substitutions, as well as planting instructions and plant adaptation maps to ensure professional results with your new landscape.

See page 157 to order your regionalized Blueprint Package.

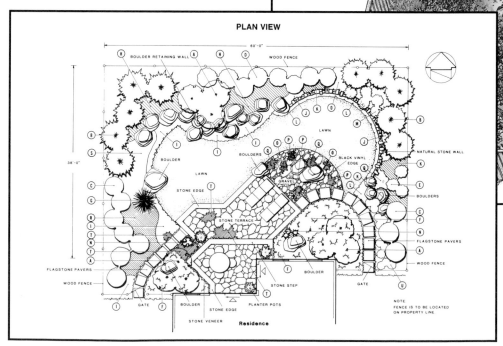

Landscape Plan L259 shown in summer
Designed by Michael J. Opisso

40

For much of its visual excitement, this dynamic design relies on the contrast between the overlapping curves of the pathway, gravel bed, and low rock wall on the right and the angles of the split-level stone terrace on the left. In arid areas, you may wish to substitute crushed granite or pea gravel for the lawn.

Water Garden

There are few places more tranquil, more relaxing, or more cooling on a hot summer day than a garden with a view of the water — even if the water is no more than a garden pool. In the garden pictured here, two ponds filled with water lilies are used to create a tranquil setting. The first pond is situated near the house, where it is visible from the indoors. The deck is cantilevered over the pond to enhance the closeness of the water, and is covered with an overhead trellis, which ties the two areas together. The trellising also frames the view of the pond from the deck, and of the deck from the garden area.

A second, smaller pond is set into the corner of the garden and has a backdrop of early-spring flowering trees, ferns, and shade-loving perennials. This intimate retreat is made complete by setting a bench and planter pots beside the pond.

Throughout the property, river-rock paving enhances the natural feeling of the water and provides a sitting area nearby for quiet contemplation. Moss rocks, placed in strategic places in the garden, further carry out the naturalistic theme, as do most of the landscape plants. The shrubs and perennials bordering the undulating lawn provide the needed soft-textured, informal look that makes both ponds seem natural and right at home.

Regionalized Plant Lists

Because climate and growing conditions vary greatly throughout North America, it is impossible to list here all the plants for this landscape plan that would do well everywhere on the continent. However, you can order a Blueprint Package with plant lists keyed to this plan and selected by expert horticulturists to thrive in your area.

The six-page Blueprint Package features a large-size version of this Plan View, plus a detailed regional Plant and Materials List. It also includes an illustrated list of hundreds of landscape plants suited to your region, in case you wish to make substitutions, as well as planting instructions and plant adaptation maps to ensure professional results with your new landscape.

See page 157 to order your regionalized Blueprint Package.

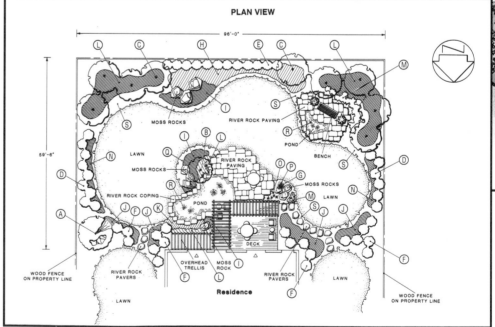

PLAN VIEW

Landscape Plan L253 shown in summer
Designed by Michael J. Opisso and Damon Scott

This backyard features not one, but two, ponds in which to dip your toes during summer's heat. If you choose to keep your shoes on, sit on the patio near the large pond or on the bench by the small one to cool off in the reflection of the colorful surroundings.

Admire your lovely woodland on a summer evening from the convenience of the raised deck, or at midday from the shaded, secluded bench in the far corner. Gentle curves, punctuated by wildflowers, boulders, and trees, invite a peaceful stroll through the woodland.

Woodland Wildflower Walk

Large trees create the woodland look of this plan, which provides exactly the right environment for the native shrubs and the delicate wildflowers and ferns that need a bit of shade to flourish. If you're lucky enough to have several large trees on site and perhaps are despairing over what to grow in their shade, this plan is your answer. If you have a sunny yard but yearn for shade, plant the largest slow-growing kinds of trees you can afford, balanced by a few fast-growing kinds. Plan on removing the faster, shorter-lived trees in a few years when the more desirable trees gain some stature. Ideal slow-growing trees to consider include native oaks and sugar maples. Fast growers that can be used to create shade and scale in a hurry include alders, poplars, and willows.

Wood-chip pathways throughout the mulched wildflower border make movement through the garden easy and inviting, creating vignettes at their corners and curves. The pond and the bridge that spans it anchor the design and lend the garden its unique character. Evergreen and deciduous trees and shrubs, including many natives, provide year-round structure.

At first, the wildflowers will grow in the spaces where you plant them, in exciting drifts of color. Over time, however, they'll mingle and reseed, creating a more natural unplanned look. Please be sure to purchase nursery-propagated wildflower plants and seeds; never transplant them from the wild or buy them from sources that gather them wild, since doing so further endangers the beauty of our natural heritage.

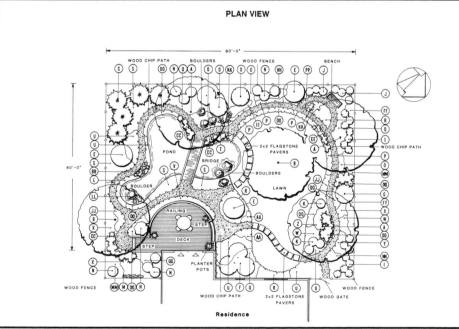

PLAN VIEW

Landscape Plan L260 shown in spring
Designed by Damon Scott and Jim Morgan

Regionalized Plant Lists

Because climate and growing conditions vary greatly throughout North America, it is impossible to list here all the plants for this landscape plan that would do well everywhere on the continent. However, you can order a Blueprint Package with plant lists keyed to this plan and selected by expert horticulturists to thrive in your area.

The six-page Blueprint Package features a large-size version of this Plan View, plus a detailed regional Plant and Materials List. It also includes an illustrated list of hundreds of landscape plants suited to your region, in case you wish to make substitutions, as well as planting instructions and plant adaptation maps to ensure professional results with your new landscape.

See page 157 to order your regionalized Blueprint Package.

An orchard and vegetable plot fits attractively into this backyard because, besides bearing apples and pears, the fruit trees also have beautiful flowers and lush foliage.

BACKYARDS FOR FOOD GARDENERS

*These Designs Will Delight the Suburban Food Gardener
Dreaming of Self-Sufficiency*

Finding an attractive way to integrate a vegetable plot or an orchard and an accompanying toolshed and compost bin is a challenge for any backyard landscaper. In all too many cases, the vegetable garden rises from the middle of the lawn, forming an unattractive rectangle of bare soil in winter and geometric rows of green plants during the growing season. Such an arrangement becomes a difficult-to-ignore eyesore, since it dominates the yard, leaving little space for other outdoor activities.

Landscape designers approach the problem of satisfying the family food gardener's space needs by first considering the landscape as a whole. Then they figure out how to attractively integrate the intensive gardening areas into a design that beautifies the property while serving other outdoor needs. The four plans in this chapter demonstrate how beautiful and effective a backyard can be, even when it's used to supply most of the family's produce needs. Each plan contains a roomy deck or patio for lounging and entertaining, and two of the plans offer outdoor kitchens, where the bounty from the garden can be cooked and served fresh.

RAISED-BED GARDENING
One way to attractively design a vegetable garden employs an arrangement of raised beds. In addition to creating a pleasing geometrical pattern that remains throughout the year, the beds make the garden easier to care for, more productive, and more compact than traditional large-plot gardens planted in rows. All these advantages are important considerations for the suburban backyard gardener.

The raised beds shown in the designs on pages 52 and 56 use pressure-treated landscape timbers, either set lengthwise on edge or cut and set on end, to hold the soil above the ground. Such timbers won't rot and, according to the Environmental Protection Agency, the chemical treatment, unlike that used for creosote-treated wood, won't leach into the soil and be taken up by the crops. However, be careful not to inhale the dust when you saw the timbers, and don't burn any scraps.

For the greatest productivity, turn over the soil at the bottom of the beds and work in copious amounts of nutrient-rich compost or rotted manure. When the beds are designed to the appropriate length and width, all the plants are within arm's reach. Since you never have to walk on the bed, the soil remains fluffy and moisture retentive. Raised beds also drain better and warm up earlier in spring than traditional plots, which means you can plant earlier and harvest sooner.

The rows between crops in traditional vegetable gardens are meant to be walked on, but, in the landscape designs offered here, you walk between the beds on mud-free, wood-chip paths. That allows you to plant the vegetables closer together than usual. For instance, if a seed packet says to space the plants 8 inches apart in rows 1½ feet apart, then set them 6 inches apart in all directions. Such close spacing means that the vegetables will shade the ground as they fill in, discouraging weeds and keeping the soil cool and moist.

EDIBLE LANDSCAPING

The new trend of edible landscaping satisfies the needs of homeowners who wish to beautify their property and grow their own food. This proves especially true for anyone with a small property or limited sunny space for growing crops. Capturing the imagination of innovative landscape designers, edible landscaping relies on using beautiful fruit trees, berry bushes, and nut trees, as well as herb and vegetable plants, in place of more traditional landscape plants. And why not? An apple tree in bloom looks just as lovely as an ornamental flowering tree, and in addition to supplying landscape beauty, it produces a crop of delicious apples.

The trick in edible landscaping is to situate the food plants in the landscape according to the artistic rules of landscape design, while still providing for the cultural needs of the crops. Here are some easy-to-follow guidelines for turning your backyard into a productive and beautiful edible landscape.

- Plant fruit and nut trees, such as apple, cherry, peach, persimmon, pecan, and Chinese chestnut, instead of traditional shade and flowering trees in the lawn and in borders.
- Arrange berry plants, such as blueberry, bush cherry, and cranberrybush viburnum, rather than traditional flowering shrubs in shrub borders.
- Use culinary herbs with colorful or attractive foliage, such as curly parsley, purple basil, and golden oregano, as accents in the flower garden.
- Plant vegetables with attractive fruit, such as hot or sweet pepper, eggplant, and tomato, as colorful additions in a border planting.
- Grow vegetables with colorful foliage or striking leaf textures, such as rhubarb, Swiss chard, kale, cabbage, and asparagus, in border plantings.
- Grow kiwi, grapes, or other fruiting vines as shade producers on decorative arbors and overhead trellises.

Not enough room to cultivate a separate vegetable garden? Try edible landscaping. This attractive border features flowers, herbs, and vegetables all growing happily together in the heat reflected off the house wall.

Fruit Tree Choices

Fruit trees used to come in one size: full-size, or standard, as it's known today. These trees grow up to 25 feet high, which makes them difficult to prune, spray, and harvest. Dwarf and semidwarf versions of the popular varieties are just as productive but bear fruit earlier than standard trees and are much easier to tend. They're recommended for home orchards because of their easy-care attributes and because their small size means that more trees will fit into an average backyard. The plans shown here use semidwarf trees because they grow tall enough to be ornamental, about 15 feet high, but are still easy to maintain.

The most crucial factor to consider in choosing fruit tree varieties is the annual minimum temperature and the duration of winter's cold. Fruit trees have a chilling requirement—a need for a certain duration of cold. Inadequately chilled trees leaf out poorly in spring and produce few if any fruits. Different varieties vary in their chilling requirement. If you order any of the plans featuring fruit trees from the designs on the following pages, be assured that the varieties will be suitable for your region. The different varieties were also selected to be compatible so they'll cross-pollinate and set fruit.

ON THE PRACTICAL SIDE

Gardening chores take less effort and time when the tools and work areas you need are right at hand. Plan to make these areas as accessible, yet as attractive, as possible. Even though you're devoting a large area to food gardening, your family and guests will find the backyard a welcoming place in which to relax rather than feel as if they're vacationing on a farm.

Storage Sheds

If you do any kind of intensive gardening, you'll be glad of a toolshed in your yard. This way, you won't have to walk back and forth constantly to the garage to get the shovel or wheelbarrow you left behind or didn't realize you needed. Situate the toolshed to the side of the yard where it doesn't take center stage but is still conveniently located. To make the structure even less obvious, you may wish to screen it partially from view with shrubbery, as several of the designs on the following pages do.

If possible, try to choose a toolshed with an attractive, yet functional, design. Ones that look like small barns complement Colonial-style homes, whereas angular redwood styles look better with contemporary architecture. Paint or stain the shed to match your home and it'll fit nicely into the landscape design. Do-it-yourselfers can order prefabricated toolshed kits ready for assembling. (See page 150 for the toolsheds featured in the designs that follow.

Compost Bins

These days fewer and fewer communities are collecting yard waste, and more and more homeowners are composting fallen leaves, grass clippings, garden trimmings, and kitchen scraps. Turning garbage into black gold to improve your soil and fertilize your plants isn't a difficult task once you master a few rules. Finding a good spot to do the alchemy may be harder.

Piling it On

A compost pile will decompose quickly if the ingredients are turned and mixed every few days or at least once a week. This so-called hot composting method takes a lot of physical labor and isn't a method for the fainthearted. Fortunately, if you don't want to turn the pile, it'll decompose slowly over six months to a year, as long as the ingredients are well mixed. For either hot or cold composting, the chemistry works best and with the least odor if you mix equal amounts of wet (green) and dry (brown) ingredients. For instance, you can mix equal amounts of dry leaves (brown) and grass clippings (green) as you build the pile.

A pile can be freestanding or contained in a bin. The advantage of a bin is that it transforms an unsightly pile into a neat-looking garden structure and keeps animals from foraging in the compost. However, the pile will "cook" just as well either way, as long as it isn't too large, too wet, or too dry. A compost pile measuring about 3 by 3 by 3 feet, or 3 cubic feet, is ideal.

Several of the landscape plans in this chapter include a place for a three-bin wood composter. (See pages 146 and 147 for construction plans.) This type of compost system works very well for cold composting. One bin contains finished compost to use during the growing season; another bin contains compost that's in the process of decomposing; and the remaining bin is ready to receive the scraps and prunings you toss into it daily. For hot composting, you can conveniently turn the pile by shifting the ingredients from one bin into the adjoining one.

If you make an unstructured compost pile, try to design a camouflage for it, such as a fence (see Plan L261 on page 50 and Plan L262 on page 52) or a shrubbery screen (see Plan L252 on page 54). That way, you can maintain the illusion that your backyard is a place of leisure, even if it isn't.

Any of the professionally designed landscapes that follow will transform your yard into a suburban food factory that not only yields baskets of fresh fruits and vegetables but also provides a pleasant place for your family and friends to enjoy fresh air and good company.

Backyard Apple Orchard

Your backyard can be both productive and beautiful if you create an edible landscape by planting attractive fruit-bearing trees and shrubs according to recognized landscape design principles. The designer arranged the fruit trees and shrubs in clusters and groups to create a lovely landscape that will fool anyone into thinking the garden was designed for its beauty alone. The delicious harvest is an added bonus.

Evergreen ground covers and swaths of summer-flowering perennials planted beneath the curving line of apple trees turns this into an ornamental planting, while providing easy access for both maintenance and harvest. The curving border defines the lawn and yard, creating a pleasing shape, yet proves to be a practical plan for fruit growing. The apple varieties selected are disease resistant, reducing the need for pest-control measures. Included are several types that will cross-pollinate and ripen their fruit at different times. The designer uses semidwarf trees because they bear earlier, are easier to harvest, and need less care than standard-sized trees.

Also featured are a nut tree to shade the deck, an island bed planted with a ground cover of strawberries and a dwarf fruit tree, and berry plants flanking the apple trees. Backyard gardeners will appreciate the handsome storage shed, where tools can be conveniently kept. Concealed behind several lengths of fencing, the compost piles are also right at hand for recycling garden and kitchen refuse into a valuable soil amendment.

Regionalized Plant Lists

Because climate and growing conditions vary greatly throughout North America, it is impossible to list here all the plants for this landscape plan that would do well everywhere on the continent. However, you can order a Blueprint Package with plant lists keyed to this plan and selected by expert horticulturists to thrive in your area.

The six-page Blueprint Package features a large-size version of this Plan View, plus a detailed regional Plant and Materials List. It also includes an illustrated list of hundreds of landscape plants suited to your region, in case you wish to make substitutions, as well as planting instructions and plant adaptation maps to ensure professional results with your new landscape.

See page 157 to order your regionalized Blueprint Package.

PLAN VIEW

Landscape Plan L261 shown in summer
Designed by Damon Scott

For prefabricated storage shed, see page 150.

50

Your friends will be surprised and delighted when you harvest baskets of delicious apples, berries, and nuts from this beautiful yard in summer and fall. The simple curved lawn and angular deck set off the surrounding orchard of fruiting trees and shrubs. Offering charming spring flowers, edible summer and fall fruits, and glorious fall foliage, here's a beautiful and productive backyard design for the practical gardener.

A spacious deck with an outdoor kitchen is effectively incorporated into this design for a medium-sized backyard. The large area devoted to vegetable gardening can produce more than enough fresh vegetables for a family of four. The lawn area, surrounded by flowering perennials and shrubs, is big enough for active play.

Vegetable Gardener's Outdoor Kitchen

Here's a wonderful plan for the serious backyard gardener and outdoor chef: a yard featuring a large, raised-bed vegetable garden and a spacious deck with an outdoor kitchen for serving and enjoying the homegrown bounty. And the plan doesn't neglect floral beauty for the sake of produce: Large patches of easy-care, long-blooming perennials catch the eye, while flowering shrubs and evergreens provide privacy and beauty.

Vegetable gardens are difficult to live with in many suburban backyards because they look barren during the off-seasons. Once the spinach, lettuce, and cabbages are harvested, it's back to bare dirt again. But this plan is designed with raised beds to provide visual structure and, at the same time, improve growing conditions by creating warmer, better-drained, and more fertile soil. The size of the beds in this garden permits easy tending because all the plants are within an arm's reach and grow closely together to discourage weeds. Wood chips cover the permanent pathways to reduce mud and improve the garden's appearance. The storage shed and compost area for recycling garden and kitchen waste are located conveniently close to the vegetable beds, but they're attractively screened by evergreens.

Connected to the entire length of the house, the large deck angles toward the vegetable garden, expanding in width as it turns. The designer repeated the deck's shape in the layout of the raised beds, enhancing the landscape's sense of unity. A countertop with a sink, a built-in barbecue, and storage space is tucked into the corner under the dappled shade of a deciduous tree.

Regionalized Plant Lists

Because climate and growing conditions vary greatly throughout North America, it is impossible to list here all the plants for this landscape plan that would do well everywhere on the continent. However, you can order a Blueprint Package with plant lists keyed to this plan and selected by expert horticulturists to thrive in your area.

The six-page Blueprint Package features a large-size version of this Plan View, plus a detailed regional Plant and Materials List. It also includes an illustrated list of hundreds of landscape plants suited to your region, in case you wish to make substitutions, as well as planting instructions and plant adaptation maps to ensure professional results with your new landscape.

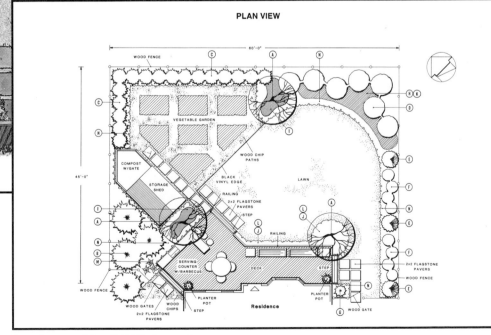

PLAN VIEW

Landscape Plan L262 shown in summer
Designed by Michael J. Opisso
For Deck Plan L120, see page 153.

See page 157 to order your regionalized Blueprint Package.

53

Edible Landscape

The suburban food gardener needn't worry about turning the backyard into unattractive rows of vegetables when following this innovative design. Here is a backyard that looks good enough to eat! It is designed to produce abundant, fresh, home-grown produce and still be a beautiful spot for relaxing and entertaining. Though the main feature of the property is a central vegetable garden, many of the landscape plants used in the border plantings and along the house produce edible fruit as well. These plants were especially chosen because they can perform double duty, acting both as ornamentals and as food-producers.

The vegetable garden is accessible by way of a short path around the lawn. The garden is designed in a round form for greater interest, and has gravel paths dissecting it for ease of working and harvesting. Even in winter, when bare of plantings, this garden will be attractive to look at because of its geometrical layout. The designer has left the choice of vegetables up to the gardener and chef, but there is plenty of space to grow the family's favorite choices. Off to the side, a storage shed provides needed space for storing wheelbarrow, hoe, and other gardening paraphernalia. A compost pile is conveniently located out of sight behind the shed.

The outdoor kitchen area on the brick patio contains a barbecue, a sink, and a serving cabinet that doubles as a bar. Covered with an overhead lattice to set off the chef's culinary preparation area, this part of the patio provides a comfortable spot in which to lounge and dine out of the sun. For sunning, move out from under the lattice and soak up the rays.

Regionalized Plant Lists

Because climate and growing conditions vary greatly throughout North America, it is impossible to list here all the plants for this landscape plan that would do well everywhere on the continent. However, you can order a Blueprint Package with plant lists keyed to this plan and selected by expert horticulturists to thrive in your area.

The six-page Blueprint Package features a large-size version of this Plan View, plus a detailed regional Plant and Materials List. It also includes an illustrated list of hundreds of landscape plants suited to your region, in case you wish to make substitutions, as well as planting instructions and plant adaptation maps to ensure professional results with your new landscape.

See page 157 to order your regionalized Blueprint Package.

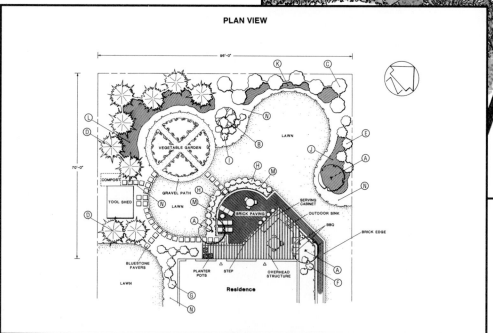

PLAN VIEW

Landscape Plan L252 shown in summer
Designed by Michael J. Opisso

A cook's garden, this backyard provides everything the family needs to eat except for the hamburgers and buns. The vegetable garden is integrated into the yard in a manner infinitely more attractive than usual vegetable gardens, and the attractive shrub borders feature berry plants and fruit trees.

Casual elegance defines the character of this garden
plan featuring a brick terrace, formal herb garden,
and raised-bed vegetable garden. Note the repeating
shapes and lines of the landscape, which create a un-
ified feeling, and the classic-style storage shed, which
turns function into beauty.

Formal Herb and Vegetable Gardens

The formal herb garden evolved as it has because the design is both functional and lovely to look at. Exuberantly spreading herbs find themselves restrained by the brick-edged beds. At the same time, the paths show off the herbs' charms and provide an attractive structure during the off-seasons. The designer chose a collection of the most useful fragrant and culinary herbs and arranged them in a pattern that enhances their colorful flowers and foliage. A central sundial, a cocoa-shell mulch emitting a delicious chocolate aroma, and a bench under the trees for relaxed viewing further accent the herb garden.

The raised-bed vegetable garden, built from attractive on-end timbers, not only creates a structure to contain the crops but also reduces the need to bend over, facilitating planting and harvesting. The area between the beds is mulched with wood chips to eliminate muddy feet and weeds. You'll appreciate the handy storage shed and efficient three-bin composter, positioned on the right.

The designer repeated the gracefully arching semicircles of the herb garden in the brick terrace and the lawn, visually linking the elements of the garden and creating a sense of unity. Likewise, the arc of flowering trees around the herb garden repeats and reinforces the same curve. The trees help enclose the garden and create privacy, while a wide variety of easy-care perennials, bulbs, and shrubs provide a long season's worth of flowering interest.

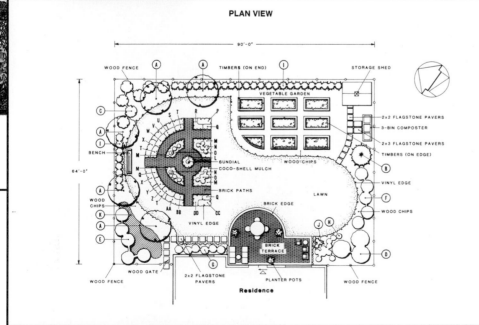

PLAN VIEW

Landscape Plan L263 shown in summer
Designed by Michael J. Opisso

For prefabricated storage shed, see page 150.
For compost bin plans, see pages 146 and 147.

Regionalized Plant Lists

Because climate and growing conditions vary greatly throughout North America, it is impossible to list here all the plants for this landscape plan that would do well everywhere on the continent. However, you can order a Blueprint Package with plant lists keyed to this plan and selected by expert horticulturists to thrive in your area.

The six-page Blueprint Package features a large-size version of this Plan View, plus a detailed regional Plant and Materials List. It also includes an illustrated list of hundreds of landscape plants suited to your region, in case you wish to make substitutions, as well as planting instructions and plant adaptation maps to ensure professional results with your new landscape.

See page 157 to order your regionalized Blueprint Package.

Family and friends will enjoy dining in the shade, lounging in the sun, and dipping in the pool in this beautiful backyard. Notice how the brick and bluestone masonry on the upper patio is repeated around the pool, linking the two areas and giving the design a spacious and elegant feeling.

BACKYARDS WITH SWIMMING POOLS

*For Floaters or Swimmers, These Designs Will
Inspire You to Build Your Very Own Pool*

Nothing provides more refreshment on a hot summer day than a cool dip in a swimming pool. And swimming is one of the best types of exercise you can do—it works all the muscles without straining the joints. If you long for a swimming pool where you can exercise and your children can play, study the designs presented in this chapter to see just how wonderful your backyard can be.

MAKING CONSTRUCTION CHOICES

Until this century, all pools, whether large or small, were rectangular. In the 1950s, new construction methods revolutionized swimming-pool design, and new shapes were introduced. With the advent of the plastics and vinyl industry, pools became affordable to most homeowners.

Pool Shapes and Sizes

In-ground pools can be built in a number of basic shapes, each of which has advantages. Select the one that best suits your backyard. Circular pools adapt well to small yards, where they're commonly used for shallow wading pools, but they can also be made deep enough for diving. Teardrop or oval pools adapt to almost any backyard. The most popular pool in recent years has been the natural, free-form shape; its gentle

curves can be modified to fit almost any spot, and the shape lends itself well to creative landscaping.

A traditional rectangular pool can be made to any proportions. If you like to swim for exercise, nothing beats a rectangular pool. A narrow lap pool, which takes up less space than a traditional rectangle, allows serious swimmers room for straight-line swimming.

An L-shaped pool will fit in a corner or around a projection of a house on a small property. Depending on the length of the sections of the L, you can still dive and get in a decent swim. If the angle is greater than the 90 degrees of a true L, the pool is more versatile for serious swimming, with no turns to make.

A free-form pool has an advantage over most other shapes—it will fit into the irregular or crowded areas that exist in so many backyards. Custom-designed for your backyard, an irregular shape can be easily integrated into an existing landscape, or a new, naturalistic landscape can be added to make the pool resemble a natural swimming hole.

Construction Materials—Vinyl Liner or Concrete

Pool walls can be made from a vinyl liner or from Gunite, the trade name for the concrete used. Five years ago, there wouldn't have been much debate about which was best—even though it cost more,

Gunite would have won hands down. That's because the older vinyl-lined pools didn't last a lifetime. The liners didn't hold up, and the wood construction needed expensive repairs or replacement every 15 years or so. In rare cases, an older vinyl-lined wood pool would collapse when the water was drained. This isn't a concern with today's vinyl-liner technology. For a time, sturdy asbestos walls replaced wood walls, eliminating the problem of rotting. In recent years, however, safety concerns about asbestos prompted the development of new methods. Asbestos construction has been replaced by galvanized steel walls, designed to last a lifetime.

An average-sized (20 by 40 feet) vinyl-lined pool costs about $10,000, without any landscaping included. (Prices are mostly for comparison purposes and can vary greatly from area to area.) The vinyl liner itself lasts about 15 years, before it needs to be replaced at a cost of about $1,500. A Gunite pool costs more to construct than a vinyl-lined pool—about $18,000 to $20,000.

A concrete pool may be a status symbol to some and worth the extra price, but don't expect it to perform any better than a modern vinyl-lined pool. The main advantage of a Gunite pool is that it can be built in unlimited shapes with varied amenities, such as a waterfall or spa, and can be custom-painted. A new technology from Australia combines Gunite with stone, creating pebbled walls.

A Gunite pool is shaped with steel, and then concrete is sprayed onto the steel framework. In the final step, marble dust is applied, giving the finish and color to the pool. Since the color is hand-mixed into the marble dust, you can get exactly the color you want. You may have to reapply marble dust every 15 years or so, at a cost of $3,000 to $4,000.

Pool Colors — the Finishing Touch

The interior color of the pool determines the appearance of the pool. A traditional white-walled pool looks bright aqua, reflecting the blue of the sky with great sparkle. A tiled pool evokes a Roman spa. Light blue or green finishes give the appearance of tinted water, whereas gray or black yields the most dramatic effect, with fantastic reflections of surrounding plants and sky giving the impression of a real pond or lake with its dark depths. A dark color retains the sun's heat, raising the water temperature and extending the season during which the water is comfortable for swimmers.

Landscape design: Margaret West

The dark paint of this Gunite pool gives the water mysterious depths while retaining more of the sun's heat than a traditional white-painted pool.

For many years, vinyl liners were available in a limited number of colors. Today, you can choose from among shades of blue, white, or gray, and even ones resembling tile. Gunite can be painted any color you wish.

SAFETY FENCING

Safety comes first when planning a pool. Many communities have ordinances requiring fencing around an in-ground pool. The laws vary—some require a fence around the pool itself (including the surrounding deck), whereas others consider a fence that encloses the property sufficient. Fence height requirements vary, as do the materials. An evergreen hedge may meet some towns' definition of a fence, and others may only accept solid wood fencing. Before proceeding, check with your local authorities to be sure your plan complies with the requirements.

INNOVATIONS IN POOL CARE

Traditionally, pool owners used chlorine to sanitize the water. Chlorine works well, but some people are sensitive to the chemical. It also ages bathing suits quickly—elastic becomes slack and colors fade. Chlorine-treated pool water, in the dilution used in home pools today, won't burn the surrounding grass or harm nearby plants if it splashes on them. However, don't use pool water for watering plants.

New alternatives to chlorine include bromide or iodine, which are in the same chemical family as chlorine. The most revolutionary alternative is copper and silver electrodes installed near the pool filter. As the water circulates, it runs through the electrodes and minute quantities of metal go into solution, sanitizing the water. The technology was originally developed by NASA for use in space. The installation costs about $1,200, but over the years you'll save more than that in the chlorine you won't have to purchase.

CREATE A BEAUTIFUL POOL SETTING

In each of the following designs, the designer created a landscape plan to complement the mood of the pool. The Naturalistic Swimming Pool (see Plan L248 on page 62) features a dark liner that gives it the appearance of a lake. The designer completes the setting with rocks, a small waterfall, and plants that look as if they would be at home around a mountain pond. By comparison, the landscaping for the Elegant Lap Pool (see Plan L264 on page 66) evokes a formal mood, as befits the elongated rectangular shape of the pool.

Plants for Poolscapes

The designers chose small trees and shrubs to provide year-round interest without littering the pool with spent flowers, pollen, or a lot of leaves. Larger trees and shrubs remain far enough away so they don't block the sun, but they're close enough to provide privacy and screening and even block noise. One or two large trees located near the deck or patio provide shade for lounging without casting the water into shade.

Since most pools are located in the sunniest part of the yard, nearby plants can dry out quickly. The glare from a pool adds to the amount of light a plant gets—a consideration when choosing plants. Drought-tolerant plants can play an important role in a pool landscape. With water consumption an issue in many areas, such plants are a logical choice to include in a poolscape. Particularly versatile are ornamental grasses, which are available in a range of heights, from edging plants less than a foot high to 10-foot-high types that provide privacy. Many are perennial, sending up attractive flowers from midsummer into fall. As the weather grows cold, the grasses turn color, some looking like pale wheat, swaying in the breeze, even holding up under the snows of winter.

Patios and Decks for Relaxing

Much of your outdoor life will revolve around the pool, so plan for a generous hardscape for lounging and entertaining. Allow places for nonswimmers to relax without getting splashed, as is done in the designs for the Elegant Lap Pool (L264 on page 66) and the Kidney-Shaped Pool (L265 on page 68.)

The patio or deck around a pool serves both functional and aesthetic purposes. It provides a safe walkway for swimmers and a necessary drainage surface in addition to framing the pool. Be generous with decking: Poolside furniture and sunbathers take up plenty of space. A rim of coping stone and a 3- or 4-foot-wide strip of concrete or brick surrounds a typical pool, but the pool will be more attractive and useful with a wide deck or patio on at least one or two sides, as is shown in the following plans. An interesting variation is to eliminate the coping stone and extend the decking or stonework right to the water's edge, as in the Naturalistic Swimming Pool (see Plan L248 on page 62), where the uninterrupted poolside surface draws the eye to the water, integrating the pool and the garden. However you arrange the patio or deck, be sure to orient it to the south or southwest if sunbathing is an important need.

When designing a backyard pool and landscape, consider who will be using the pool. Will it be primarily for serious swimmers or for family fun and games? The landscape plans presented on the following pages demonstrate a variety of ways to incorporate a swimming pool into a backyard. One of these designs may be just the ticket for you and your family.

Naturalistic Swimming Pool

If you look at this landscape design and ask yourself, "Is that really a swimming pool?" then the designer is to be congratulated because he has succeeded in his intention. Yes, it *is* a swimming pool, but the pool looks more like a natural pond and waterfall — one that you might discover in a clearing in the woods during a hike in the wilderness.

The designer achieves this aesthetically pleasing, natural look by employing several techniques. He creates the pool in an irregular free-form shape and paints it "black," actually a very dark marine blue, to suggest the depths of a lake. Large boulders form the waterfalls, one of which falls from a holding pond set among the boulders. River rock paving, the type of water-worn rocks that line the cool water of a natural spring or a rushing stream, surrounds the front of the pool. The far side of the pool is planted right to the edge, blending the pool into the landscape. If you want to make a splash, you can even dive into this pool — from a diving rock rather than a diving board.

Although the pool is the main attraction here, the rest of the landscape offers a serene setting with abundant floral and foliage interest throughout the year. For security reasons, a wooden stockade fence surrounds the entire backyard, yet the plantings camouflage it well. The irregular kidney shape of the lawn is pleasing to look at and beautifully integrates the naturalistic pool and landscaping into its man-made setting.

Regionalized Plant Lists

Because climate and growing conditions vary greatly throughout North America, it is impossible to list here all the plants for this landscape plan that would do well everywhere on the continent. However, you can order a Blueprint Package with plant lists keyed to this plan and selected by expert horticulturists to thrive in your area.

The six-page Blueprint Package features a large-size version of this Plan View, plus a detailed regional Plant and Materials List. It also includes an illustrated list of hundreds of landscape plants suited to your region, in case you wish to make substitutions, as well as planting instructions and plant adaptation maps to ensure professional results with your new landscape.

See page 157 to order your regionalized Blueprint Package.

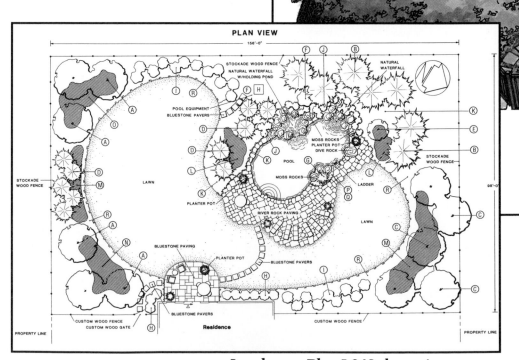

Landscape Plan L248 shown in summer
Designed by Damon Scott

Resembling a tranquil country pond high in the mountains, this swimming pool, with its waterfalls, river-rock paving, and border plantings, brings a wonderful, natural setting to your own backyard.

Pool and Deck Garden

Take the usual rectangular backyard and place in it a simple rectangular swimming pool and the result, more often than not, is boring! Not so with this effective landscape design. By situating the pool along the diagonals of the property, the designer creates an exciting view that juxtaposes the angles of the hardscape with the curves of the planting areas, making the property appear larger and visually interesting.

The steps leading into the pool are placed on the outside of the rectangle to alleviate some of the straight lines; however, the theme still remains angular. This is reinforced by the lines of the wooden decking surrounding the pool. At the end of the pool, hedges not only complete the angular design, they also screen the pool's filter and heater. The line of the hedge is strengthened by two flowering trees positioned at each end; these also terminate the sight line along the pool's length.

Three planters play important roles in the planting design — they serve as pockets of color to break up the large expanse of wood. One brings color to the poolside; a second links the poolside deck with the upper deck off the house; the third wraps around the upper deck and defines the seating area. Notice how the boards change direction from one deck level to the next. Besides being visually interesting, this helps to distinguish the different use areas of the decking. The area closest to the house offers a perfect place for cooking, dining, and entertaining, while the lower deck caters to swimming and relaxing in the sun.

Regionalized Plant Lists

Because climate and growing conditions vary greatly throughout North America, it is impossible to list here all the plants for this landscape plan that would do well everywhere on the continent. However, you can order a Blueprint Package with plant lists keyed to this plan and selected by expert horticulturists to thrive in your area.

The six-page Blueprint Package features a large-size version of this Plan View, plus a detailed regional Plant and Materials List. It also includes an illustrated list of hundreds of landscape plants suited to your region, in case you wish to make substitutions, as well as planting instructions and plant adaptation maps to ensure professional results with your new landscape.

See page 157 to order your regionalized Blueprint Package.

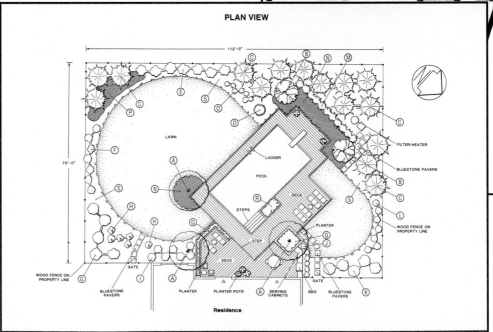

Landscape Plan L247 shown in summer
Designed by Michael J. Opisso

64

Is it possible to start with the same ingredients and combine them into a different recipe? Yes, by angling a rectangular pool, breaking up the large expanse of deck with planters, and mixing in gracefully curving shrub borders, this pool and deck garden becomes a gourmet treat.

Even modest-sized backyards have room for a lap pool for the athletically minded and those seeking only a refreshing dip. This elegant backyard plan incorporates a lovely patio and pool with a generous lawn, evergreens for privacy, flowering trees and shrubs for spring beauty, and many kinds of colorful, long-blooming perennials for a summer show.

Elegant Lap Pool

Designed primarily for exercise, a lap pool is much longer than wide, although it allows two people to swim comfortably side by side. It's also shallower than pools designed for high diving. This long, narrow pool fits economically into a small backyard, because it takes up less space and costs less to build. Although intended for a healthy workout, the pool will certainly provide cooling relief from sultry summer days for all family members, not just the athletically minded.

The lap pool not only serves as a recreational feature, but it also organizes the space in the landscape, acting as the main point of interest. The designer situated the pool easily within the confines of a modest-sized backyard by locating it off-center and at the focal point of a line of sight leading between two oval flowering trees and ending with a small specimen tree on the other side of the pool. The brick patio offsets the visual weight of the pool, balancing the design. The designer worked to vary the pattern and direction in the brick paving around the rectangular, hard-edged shape of the 35- by 10-foot pool to avoid an overly formal result.

A path of flagstone pavers, leading from the gate to the brick terrace and from the terrace to the pool, provides easy circulation through the landscape. Swimmers can reach the pool from two doors of the house. Although the perimeter plantings ensure privacy for the swimmers, a variety of flowering shrubs and perennials creates a spring-through-fall display of flower and leaf color for all to enjoy.

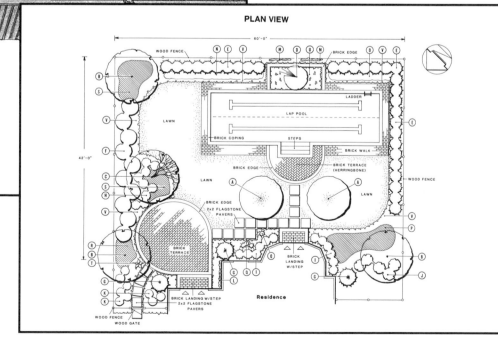

Landscape Plan L264 shown in spring
Designed by Tom Nordloh

Regionalized Plant Lists

Because climate and growing conditions vary greatly throughout North America, it is impossible to list here all the plants for this landscape plan that would do well everywhere on the continent. However, you can order a Blueprint Package with plant lists keyed to this plan and selected by expert horticulturists to thrive in your area.

The six-page Blueprint Package features a large-size version of this Plan View, plus a detailed regional Plant and Materials List. It also includes an illustrated list of hundreds of landscape plants suited to your region, in case you wish to make substitutions, as well as planting instructions and plant adaptation maps to ensure professional results with your new landscape.

See page 157 to order your regionalized Blueprint Package.

Kidney-Shaped Pool

The simplicity of the curving lines in this design helps create a private backyard of informal grace. Cornerless and nondirectional, the sensual lines of the pool emphasize neither its width nor its length. As a result, the garden's sense of space is enhanced by forcing the eye to scan the beautifully planted edges. To further connect the pool to the landscape, the shapes of the brick terrace, wood deck, lawn, stepping-stone path, and two bermed areas bordering the lawn echo the sensual pattern.

In addition to the sound-buffering berms, the groupings of background trees behind and across from the pool enhance the sense of seclusion and privacy. The designer specified three vase-shaped, deciduous shade trees for the garden to balance the visual weight of the pool. Needled evergreens provide privacy by wrapping around the rear corner of the property behind the pool. Note the specimen shrub planted on the pool's edge and set off against the dark foliage of the evergreens: The gracefully spreading plant makes a spectacular sight when in bloom in spring and again in fall and winter when colorful fruits decorate its branches.

Blooming just in advance of the flowering tree near the pool are three equally spectacular small flowering trees along the patio; these are located near the house for maximum enjoyment because the weather may still be chilly in early spring. Extravagant patches of long-blooming perennials provide color during the summer months, when you'll be outside enjoying the pool and the generous outdoor living space.

Regionalized Plant Lists

Because climate and growing conditions vary greatly throughout North America, it is impossible to list here all the plants for this landscape plan that would do well everywhere on the continent. However, you can order a Blueprint Package with plant lists keyed to this plan and selected by expert horticulturists to thrive in your area.

The six-page Blueprint Package features a large-size version of this Plan View, plus a detailed regional Plant and Materials List. It also includes an illustrated list of hundreds of landscape plants suited to your region, in case you wish to make substitutions, as well as planting instructions and plant adaptation maps to ensure professional results with your new landscape.

See page 157 to order your regionalized Blueprint Package.

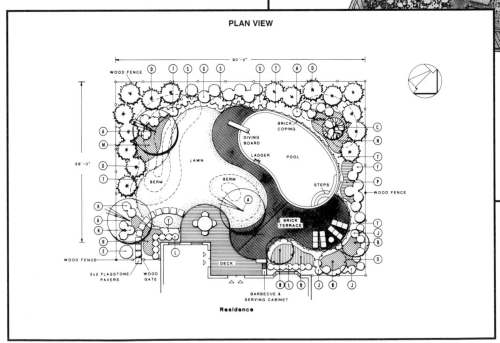

Landscape Plan L265 shown in summer
Designed by Tom Nordloh

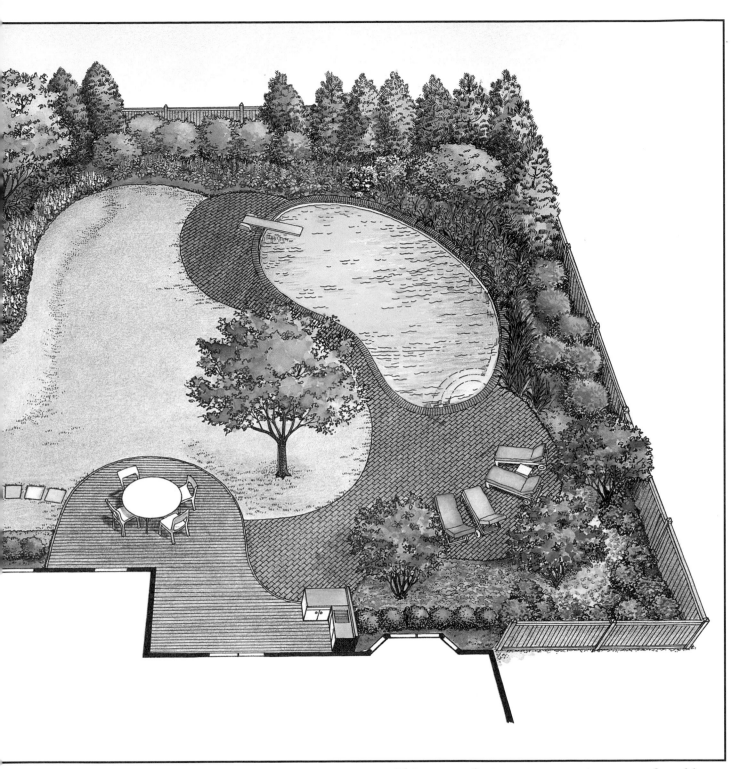

This serene design creates a private, comfortable, quiet, and carefree mood for relaxing with family and friends. Vase-shaped shade trees block the hot sun on the deck and patio while letting the sun warm the swimming pool.

A small lawn, plants chosen for suitability to the site and for slow rate of growth, and well-mulched planting beds mean that this pretty yard practically takes care of itself.

LOW-MAINTENANCE BACKYARD DESIGNS

Easy-Care Landscapes Allow You to Enjoy Your Yard Rather Than Fuss Over It

Agardener once said that the only maintenance-free garden he ever saw was a stretch of solid concrete painted green. No maintenance perhaps, but not particularly attractive either. The definition of low maintenance is certainly subjective—someone who hates to work outdoors may consider a yard needing one hour of attention a week low maintenance, whereas an avid gardener may consider six hours a week undemanding. Only you know how much time you wish to devote to caring for your yard and garden.

The low-maintenance plans featured in this chapter are a far cry from green concrete, yet they don't take much care on a weekly or even monthly basis. The designers considered the maintenance needs of the yards when creating these designs, making conscious choices to reduce the work involved in keeping the yards healthy and attractive. When designing your own low-maintenance yard, consider the following work-saving tips from the professionals.

- Reduce the size of the lawn; replace turf with ground covers, hardscape, or mulched shrub borders.
- Apply organic mulch, such as wood chips, thickly under permanent plantings to reduce the need to water and weed.
- Plant dwarf or slow-growing varieties of shrubs that won't need routine pruning to keep them in bounds.
- Choose trees with compound leaves made up of tiny leaflets to make fall raking an easy chore.
- Underplant trees with ground covers that absorb fallen leaves and debris to reduce cleanup.
- Install weed barriers beneath gravel, paving, or mulch to prevent weeds.
- Keep to a minimum unconnected lawn areas and specimen plantings in the lawn to ease mowing chores.
- Install permanent borders or edgings between the lawn and planting beds to eliminate the need to trim lawn edges and to keep grass out of shrub and flower beds.
- Choose easy-care, long-lived perennials and flowering shrubs rather than high-maintenance annuals to provide floral beauty.
- Choose disease-resistant, well-adapted plants that don't need constant pest-proofing, watering, pruning, staking, or other pampering to thrive.

LOW MAINTENANCE CAN BE BEAUTIFUL

Just because it's easy to care for doesn't mean your backyard can't be beautiful. A low-maintenance garden can be just as stunning as a high-maintenance yard. Decide first what type of landscape you wish to have, then approach the design with work-saving in mind. Do you want a lush-looking garden in soft greens and blues, or do you prefer bolder colors? Is a lawn an integral part of your idea of a backyard, or can another flooring be substituted? Do you prefer simple lines and a tailored look, or do you like an untamed naturalistic appearance? Does the idea of a garden conjure up a vision of a few well-chosen specimen plants, perhaps as focal points, or a wide variety of plant material spread throughout the yard? Are you the type of person who can't walk through a garden without stopping to smell all the flowers? Do you live in one of the increasing number of communities where water has become a major consideration?

Your responses to these questions will help you decide which of the low-maintenance designs presented in this chapter is most suitable for you and your family.

GOOD-BYE LAWN, HELLO GROUND COVER

The ideal lawn is a vast swathe of verdant green that ties the landscape together, but keeping it that way is a time-consuming matter. A lawn is the biggest thief of time in any garden. It seemingly requires constant attention: No sooner have you turned your back than the grass needs another mowing, liming, or fertilizing, or the grubs have eaten it, or a fungus has invaded it. Left to its own devices, a lawn can survive without watering during the heat of summer—it simply goes dormant—but, unfortunately, brown lawns aren't in vogue during July and August.

You can still create that cool greenbelt feeling in your backyard by reducing the lawn to a more manageable size, as is done in the plans on the following pages. Lawns of 3,000 to 5,000 square feet are large enough to look nice while being small enough to be easily cared for. You might also consider planting a low-maintenance grass variety—one that grows slowly and resists drought. Buffalo grass, one such grass native to arid regions of the midwestern and western United States, has been recently introduced for use in lawns. (See page 76.)

By installing a steel or vinyl lawn edging or a brick mowing strip between the lawn and garden beds, you can keep the two areas separate. The lawn will stay on its side of the border and creeping ground covers on their side. This translates into less weeding for you, and a neater look without the time-consuming—and sometimes back-breaking—chore of edging the lawn. When properly installed so the lawn mower wheels glide right over the edging or mowing strip, you won't have to go back with a hand clipper or string-trimmer to cut scraggly edges—another great time-saver.

Alternatives to Lawn

Look to other ground-hugging plants instead of lawn grass to provide a low-maintenance green color. Good choices include evergreen plants, such as periwinkle (myrtle), English ivy, mondograss, pachysandra, wintercreeper, and prostrate juniper.

Besides looking pretty, a brick mowing strip serves two practical functions: It prevents grass roots from entering planting beds, reducing weeding tasks; and the strip allows the mower's wheels to ride over it, cutting the edges of the lawn and eliminating the need to hand-trim.

Plant these in large swathes around the borders of a greatly reduced lawn, or replace the lawn entirely with the ground cover. If you need access through the area to a patio, gate, or garden, provide stepping-stones as a path through the planting.

Replacing all or part of a lawn with gravel, stones, or sand creates a naturalistic look that's easy to care for. You can purchase different sizes of gravel or stones to create whatever feeling you want in the garden. You may wish to vary and combine them in the same garden, but keep in mind that small stones are easier to walk on and dark colors look better than light colors, which become too conspicuous. You may decide to use a band of black river stones to emulate flowing water and a strip of boulder-studded sand to create a beach in a Japanese-style garden. Be sure to use landscape fabric, or geotextile, under the stones or sand to prevent weeds from growing up from the underlying soil and to allow water to drain through to tree and shrub roots underneath.

You don't have to pave over the backyard, but increasing the hardscape in your garden also increases the usable outdoor living space while reducing maintenance. Add a deck or patio, or expand an existing one, using attractive materials, such as mortared brick, bluestone, or redwood that you allow to weather to a silvery gray. The Fragrant Shrub Garden (see Plan L267 on page 78) features a small lawn and expansive areas of deck and patio, which create a lovely, yet easy-care, design.

Imitation Meadows

Ornamental grasses rank high on the list of ideal low-maintenance plants. Highly adaptable, they grow in almost any type of soil and are attractive throughout the year. In spring, they quickly grow to their full height and volume. Their long leaves gently sway in summer breezes, and, by late summer, the plants send up spikes or plumes of flowers, which form attractive seed heads by fall. As the temperature drops, their green foliage fades to bright beige, almond, or wheat for the winter, and the dried foliage and flowers of most types remain standing through winter, providing architectural interest.

You can create an imitation or stylized meadow or prairie, such as the Naturalistic Grass Garden (see Plan L246 on page 80) by mass-planting several varieties of ornamental grass. Although it relies on nonnative plants, it looks natural and is an easy-care alternative to other types of landscape designs. The only maintenance most grasses need is to be cut to the ground in spring, just as new growth begins. A few of the tall grasses that may flatten somewhat after a heavy downpour will benefit from staking or a support put in place in spring.

MULCH MAKES A DIFFERENCE

Once you've planted your low-maintenance garden, mulch it well with wood chips, shredded leaves, or another attractive organic material to further reduce the garden chores. The importance of mulching can't be overemphasized. Not only does a 3-inch layer of mulch cut down drastically on weeds in shrub borders and flower beds, but it also insulates the soil and keeps moisture in so you don't have to water as frequently. Where ground covers will eventually blanket the soil and crowd out most weeds, you may still wish to apply an initial layer of mulch to combat weeds until the new planting fills in.

Mulch shouldn't go right up against the stem or trunk of any plant, but rather it should remain 1 or 2 inches from the base. When piled right up against a plant, mulch can smother the lower stem or cause it to rot. An organic mulch eventually decays, adding beneficial material and nutrients to the soil, and needs to be refreshed every year or so. Black plastic mulch doesn't let rain into the soil and isn't recommended for use beneath shrubs and trees. However, it does make a good choice for vegetable beds if you can install an irrigation system beneath the plastic.

In the low-maintenance plans illustrated in this chapter, the designers carefully selected plants that are easy to maintain and usually free of diseases and insects. By relying on such plants to carry out the low-maintenance designs, these lovely gardens will leave you with practically no yard work at all.

When you choose a low-maintenance backyard design, such as any of those on the following pages, you'll be assured of having a beautiful yard that you can truly enjoy because its beauty doesn't come at the expense of hours of your labor.

Mulching your garden's soil with a thick covering of organic matter, such as the pine needles used in this flower border, reduces later weeding, watering, and fertilizing chores, because the mulch smothers weeds, keeps the soil cool and moist, and slowly decomposes, releasing its nutrients.

Landscape design: Conni Cross

Japanese-Style Garden

When a busy couple desires a garden that is distinctive and requires little maintenance, the Japanese-style garden and backyard pictured here are a perfect solution. The essence of a Japanese garden lies in emulating nature through simple, clean lines that do not look contrived. The low, tight hedges underscore the planting behind them, while providing a contrast in form. Looking straight out from the deck, the perimeter planting is a harmony of shades of green, with interest provided from contrasting textures. Plants throughout require little fuss.

Paving stones border the deck because, in the Japanese garden, every element has both an aesthetic and a functional purpose. The stones alleviate the wear that would result from stepping directly onto the lawn from the deck, and provide a visual transition between the man-made deck and the natural grass. The pavers act as more than a path; they also provide a sight line to the stone lantern on the left side of the garden.

The deck, like the rest of the landscape, has clean, simple lines, and provides the transition from the home's interior to the garden. It surrounds a viewing garden, one step down. In the Japanese tradition, this miniature landscape mimics a natural scene. The one large moss rock plays an important role—it is situated at the intersection of the stepping-stone paths that lead through the garden; here a decision must be made as to which way to turn. The stone water basin, a symbolic part of the Japanese tea ceremony, is located near the door to the house, signaling the entrance to a very special place.

Regionalized Plant Lists

Because climate and growing conditions vary greatly throughout North America, it is impossible to list here all the plants for this landscape plan that would do well everywhere on the continent. However, you can order a Blueprint Package with plant lists keyed to this plan and selected by expert horticulturists to thrive in your area.

The six-page Blueprint Package features a large-size version of this Plan View, plus a detailed regional Plant and Materials List. It also includes an illustrated list of hundreds of landscape plants suited to your region, in case you wish to make substitutions, as well as planting instructions and plant adaptation maps to ensure professional results with your new landscape.

See page 157 to order your regionalized Blueprint Package.

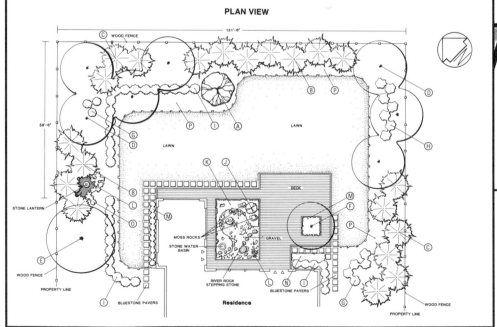

PLAN VIEW

Landscape Plan L241 shown in spring
Designed by Michael J. Opisso

74

This beautiful Japanese-style garden provides space for outdoor living and entertaining in a tranquil setting. Featuring straight, simple lines, a small lawn, a large deck, and extensive plantings of ground covers and evergreens, the garden practically cares for itself.

Drought-Tolerant Garden

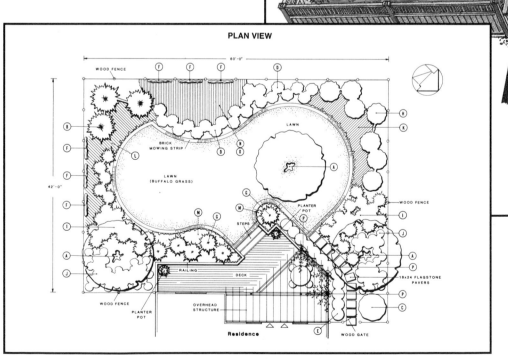

This design proves that drought tolerance and low maintenance don't have to be boring. This attractive backyard looks lush, colorful, and inviting, but it relies entirely on plants that flourish even if water is scarce. That means you won't spend much time tending to their watering needs once the plantings are established. Even the lawn is planted with a newly developed turf grass that tolerates long periods of drought.

For the lawn the designer specified buffalo grass, a native grass of the American West. The grass has fine-textured, grayish green leaf blades, tolerates cold, and needs far less water than usual lawns to remain green and healthy. It goes completely dormant during periods of extended drought but greens up with rain or irrigation. To keep the lawn green throughout summer, all you need to do is water occasionally if rainfall doesn't cooperate. And mowing is an occasional activity, too! This slow-growing grass needs mowing to about 1 inch high only several times in summer. To keep the grass from spreading into the planting borders—and to reduce weeding and edging chores—the designer called for a decorative brick mowing strip surrounding the lawn.

Deciduous and evergreen trees and shrubs interplanted with long-blooming flowering perennials, all of them drought tolerant, adorn the yard, bringing color every season. Against the fence grow espaliered shrubs, which offer flowers in spring and berries in winter. The vine-covered trellis shades the roomy, angular deck, where you can sit in cool seclusion and relax while your beautiful backyard takes care of itself.

Regionalized Plant Lists

Because climate and growing conditions vary greatly throughout North America, it is impossible to list here all the plants for this landscape plan that would do well everywhere on the continent. However, you can order a Blueprint Package with plant lists keyed to this plan and selected by expert horticulturists to thrive in your area.

The six-page Blueprint Package features a large-size version of this Plan View, plus a detailed regional Plant and Materials List. It also includes an illustrated list of hundreds of landscape plants suited to your region, in case you wish to make substitutions, as well as planting instructions and plant adaptation maps to ensure professional results with your new landscape.

See page 157 to order your regionalized Blueprint Package.

PLAN VIEW

Landscape Plan L266 shown in summer
Designed by Damon Scott
For Deck Plan D115, see page 152.

76

This environmentally sound landscape plan won't strain the local water supply or burden you with gardening chores, because all the plants used here—from lawn to flowers to trees—are easy-care, trouble-free kinds that flourish without frequent rain or irrigation. A wood-chip mulch blankets the ground beneath the shrubs and perennials, conserving soil moisture and smothering weeds.

In this romantic garden devoted to especially sweet-smelling shrubs, you'll find special corners—an arbor, a patio, and a wooden bench—isolated for your pleasure. The repeated curves of the lawn, patio, and paths create a harmonious and restful design, where family and friends can enjoy the delightful sights and scents permeating the air.

Fragrant Shrub Garden

I f you're the kind of gardener who always buries your nose in the nearest blossom and feels disappointed to find a gorgeous rose as scentless as it is beautiful, this landscape plan may be just the one for you. The designer made every effort to choose the most fragrant plants available to fill this low-maintenance garden with sweet and spicy aromas from spring through fall.

Curving paths and romantic, secluded sitting areas invite you to stroll and rest among the scented plants. Sit under the arbor and enjoy the intensely fragrant flowering shrubs directly behind you in spring and the heady scent of climbing roses overhead in summer. In fall, the delicate perfume of the late bloomers will delight you. Even if you don't move from the patio, the sweet, pervasive perfume of the inconspicuous flowers of the surrounding shrubs will astound you on warm July evenings.

And you'll find the garden is as easy to care for as it is fragrant, because the designer selected low-maintenance shrubs (including many dwarf types), trees, and ground covers, instead of labor-intensive annuals and perennials to provide color and fragrance. The carefully arranged shrubs have plenty of room to grow without crowding each other or outgrowing their space, so you don't have to worry about extensive pruning chores. Much of the area that would be lawn in most yards is given here to the brick patio and shrub borders, allowing more kinds of plants to be included in the landscape and minimizing lawn-care chores. Maintaining this landscape proves to be surprisingly easy—it doesn't require you to make it your life's work, even though it may look as if you have.

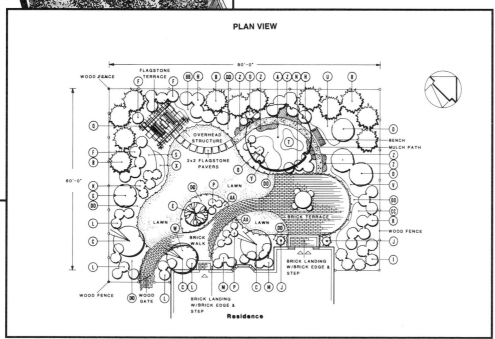

PLAN VIEW

Landscape Plan L267 shown in spring
Designed by Tom Nordloh

For arbor plan, see page 149.

Regionalized Plant Lists

Because climate and growing conditions vary greatly throughout North America, it is impossible to list here all the plants for this landscape plan that would do well everywhere on the continent. However, you can order a Blueprint Package with plant lists keyed to this plan and selected by expert horticulturists to thrive in your area.

The six-page Blueprint Package features a large-size version of this Plan View, plus a detailed regional Plant and Materials List. It also includes an illustrated list of hundreds of landscape plants suited to your region, in case you wish to make substitutions, as well as planting instructions and plant adaptation maps to ensure professional results with your new landscape.

See page 157 to order your regionalized Blueprint Package.

Low in maintenance requirements, high in natural
appeal, this garden of ornamental grasses delights
the senses all year with subdued foliage colors,
sparkling flower plumes, and rustling leaves.

Naturalistic Grass Garden

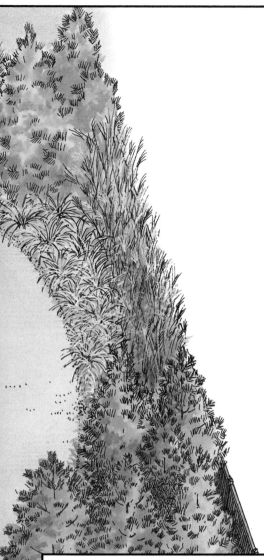

Many cultures seem to have an identifiable garden style—there are formal Italian fountain gardens, French parterres, English perennial borders, and Japanese contemplation gardens. For many years, we didn't have an American-style garden. Now, a new trend has arisen, which the originators have dubbed the "New American Garden." This style of landscaping is naturalistic and relies on sweeps of ornamental grasses to create the feel of the prairies that once dominated much of the American landscape.

The backyard garden presented here follows that theme. The grasses used vary from low-growing plants hugging the borders to tall plants reaching 6 feet or more. Some of the grasses are bold and upright; others arching and graceful. When the grasses flower, they produce plumes that dance in the wind and sparkle in the sun. Foliage colors include bright green, blue-green, variegated, and even blood red. During autumn, foliage and flowers dry in place, forming a stunning scene of naturalistic hues in varying shades of straw, almond, brown, and rust. Most of the grasses remain interesting to look at all winter, unless heavy snow flattens them to the ground. In early spring, the dried foliage must be cut off and removed to make way for new growth — but this is the only maintenance chore required by an established garden of ornamental grasses!

The design includes a large realistic-looking pond, which can be made from a vinyl liner or concrete. A the end of the path leading from the bridge, a small seating area provides a retreat.

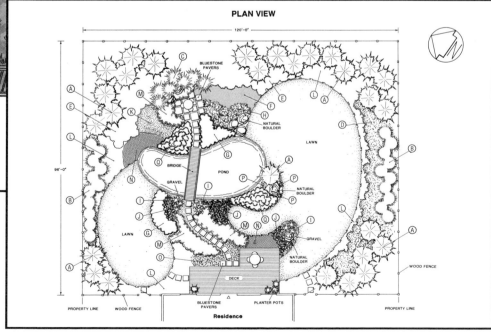

PLAN VIEW

Landscape Plan L246 shown in summer
Designed by Damon Scott

Regionalized Plant Lists

Because climate and growing conditions vary greatly throughout North America, it is impossible to list here all the plants for this landscape plan that would do well everywhere on the continent. However, you can order a Blueprint Package with plant lists keyed to this plan and selected by expert horticulturists to thrive in your area.

The six-page Blueprint Package features a large-size version of this Plan View, plus a detailed regional Plant and Materials List. It also includes an illustrated list of hundreds of landscape plants suited to your region, in case you wish to make substitutions, as well as planting instructions and plant adaptation maps to ensure professional results with your new landscape.

See page 157 to order your regionalized Blueprint Package.

Lovely Lawnless Backyard

If you feel like a weekend slave to your lawn and yard, here's a way out. Do away with the green growing grass, discard the lawn mower, and relax on the weekends. Enjoy your backyard as a peaceful haven instead of a nagging maintenance chore.

It's true that a lawn acts as an important design feature by creating a plain that carries the eye through the garden, establishing connections between the various garden elements and providing an open feeling while attractively covering the ground. However, it requires time and money to maintain. Other materials or plants that require less care can provide a similar effect. Japanese gardens often feature carefully raked gravel to mimic ocean waves; in the Southwest, prettily colored crushed granite covers many yards; in other areas, low evergreen ground covers substitute for lawn grass. In this low-maintenance backyard, the designer incorporated a large deck and patio flanked by a lakelike expanse of dark gravel where a lawn might be. A water-permeable landscape fabric underpins the layer of gravel to help halt weeds.

Tall evergreen trees along the rear boundary guarantee privacy, while three large deciduous trees provide plenty of summer shade for the deck and patio. The angular deck features an interesting cut-out space for a small viewing garden. The deck steps down to a grade-level brick patio with a circular shape that complements the gravel expanse and the planting beds. From the brick terrace a flagstone pathway leads to a bench positioned in the midst of a bed of flowering perennials. From there, you can reflect upon your garden, your house, and your free time.

Regionalized Plant Lists

Because climate and growing conditions vary greatly throughout North America, it is impossible to list here all the plants for this landscape plan that would do well everywhere on the continent. However, you can order a Blueprint Package with plant lists keyed to this plan and selected by expert horticulturists to thrive in your area.

The six-page Blueprint Package features a large-size version of this Plan View, plus a detailed regional Plant and Materials List. It also includes an illustrated list of hundreds of landscape plants suited to your region, in case you wish to make substitutions, as well as planting instructions and plant adaptation maps to ensure professional results with your new landscape.

See page 157 to order your regionalized Blueprint Package.

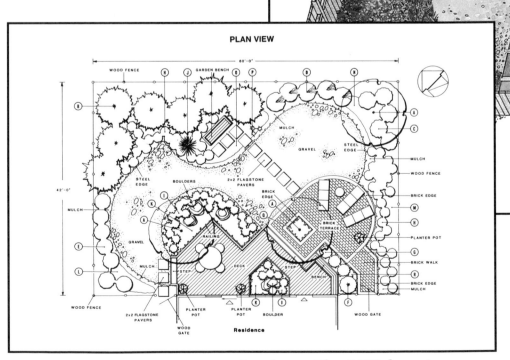

Landscape Plan L268 shown in summer
Designed by Michael J. Opisso

Eliminate the lawn, and the most time-consuming part of a gardener's maintenance routine is eliminated as well. Easy-care hard surfaces—a gravel bed, wood deck, and brick patio—take the place of the lawn, providing inviting spaces for relaxing and enjoying the surrounding flowers and greenery.

This cottage garden of fragrant flowering herbs owes its tidiness to a design featuring wood-edged beds and gravel walks.

BACKYARDS FOR FLOWER GARDENERS

These Designs Will Enchant Both Serious Flower Gardeners and Their Nongardening Family Members

The landscape plans presented in this chapter are designed especially for the serious flower lover. If you enjoy growing flowers, one of these backyard designs, each of which features a special flower garden, should be perfect for you. Choose among a variety of backyards: a formal rose garden, cottage garden, cut-flower garden, fragrance garden, or raised perennial border. The designer of each plan skillfully combines a beautiful, specialty flower garden with the rest of the backyard to create a livable landscape for the entire family to enjoy.

DESIGNING YOUR FLOWER GARDEN

Any area of your property that gets plenty of sun could work as the location for a flower garden. When designing the garden, decide what effect you're after. You may want a garden that you can walk right into from the house or patio, the way you can with the Cottage Garden (see Plan L250 on page 88). Or you may prefer to sit on the patio adjacent to the house and enjoy the view of a beautiful, flower-filled garden from across the lawn, as you can with the Raised Perennial Border (see Plan L251 on page 90) and the Fragrance Garden (see Plan L269 on page 94). Or you may enjoy strolling among the flowers, as you can in the Formal Rose Garden (see Plan L254 on page 92.)

Enclosures Set a Mood

By simply enclosing a garden, you alter its setting and mood. For example, by surrounding the garden and patio in the Cottage Garden with a white picket fence, the designer created the romantic feel of a country garden. The fence with the two arbor gates leading into the Cut-Flower Garden evokes the same mood. Fencing also serves to provide a modicum of privacy and can support flowering vines, while adding horizontal and vertical lines to the landscape. Most importantly, the fence unifies the house and garden when they're constructed of complementary materials.

The low stone wall in the Raised Perennial Border not only brings the garden up to eye level, heightening its impact, but also creates a rustic, bucolic mood for the backyard. A rock wall makes a particularly attractive feature for trailing plants to drape down. Rock-garden plants placed at the top can cascade downward, softening the wall and spreading flowers over a pretty backdrop. You can also add pockets of soil between the stones and insert small rock-garden plants to peek out from the crevices.

If your site doesn't have a natural slope to retain with a wall, you can build one with a truckload of soil. This method may be a real work-saver if your garden soil is poor—either too sandy or too heavy. Instead of having to till the poor soil and improve it with drastic amounts of organic matter, you can simply have a load of good, clean topsoil dumped behind the stone wall and—*presto!*—you have instant good garden soil to create the garden of your dreams.

Anchoring Tactics

A flower garden may look odd if you just plop it in the middle of a landscape without visually linking it to the rest of the design. You can easily integrate an island bed into the overall landscape by echoing the shape of the garden with the shape of the shrub borders, as the designer does in the Fragrance Garden. The curve of the island bed follows the same flowing lines as the rest of the landscape, creating harmony. And, likewise, the straight sides and symmetrical placement of the rose garden within the landscape of the Formal Rose Garden works effectively.

Notice that each of the backyard designs in this chapter calls for an evergreen background. Evergreens create a richly textured backdrop for the rest of the garden and provide year-round color. In the Formal Rose Garden, the roses themselves are enclosed by well-manicured, low-growing evergreen hedges, setting a very formal mood for the garden but also camouflaging the legs of the rosebushes.

Planting Flowers for Visual Impact

A single plant or flower can get easily lost in a landscape, whereas a large grouping, or mass planting, catches the eye from a distance, drawing your interest by its color or form. This is especially true with garden flowers. That's why the designer planted large drifts of a single type of flower in front of the shrubbery in the Cottage Garden. Since the enclosed garden is for close-up viewing, smaller groups of flowers seem appropriate there—but, for long-distance viewing, you'll find the most enjoyment in a large sweep of the same flowers.

Select flower colors that complement other landscape features and any woody plants that bloom at the same time. For example, a large expanse of late pink 'Maytime' tulips on one side of the landscape would complement a grouping of pink flowering weigela on the other side. You don't have to place

Brightening the edges of a backyard stream, deep-hued perennials provide an ever-changing show of flowers and foliage.

Landscape design: Thomas and Martina Rheinhart

the same types of flowering plants right in front of one another, but try to carry the color throughout the landscape.

Designing a View

Try to design and place your flower garden so that it looks as attractive from a distance as it does close up and perhaps from several points in the landscape. A patio makes a good vantage point, drawing you toward the garden. You may also want to view the flowers from indoors. In the Raised Perennial Border, the designer incorporated two main viewing positions within the landscape—looking up to the raised border from the patio, and a closer but level view into the flowers and trees from the gazebo. Such views add interest in the garden. Try to identify the possible viewing points, before situating the garden.

FORMAL OR INFORMAL

To suit our more casual lifestyles, today's landscapes and gardens are more informally designed than those of years past. But that doesn't mean there's no place for formality in the garden. Your personal taste and requirements will help you decide whether you want a formal or an informal garden.

A formal garden is usually laid out geometrically and symmetrically— it could be described as neat and precise. Lines are straight and edges square. Brick or masonry walls, terraces, fountains, statuary, topiary, and sheared hedges are at home there. A formal garden usually includes a well-manicured lawn of lavish proportions and may emphasize restful greenery over colorful flowers. The Formal Rose Garden (see Plan L254 on page 92) is an example of such a style.

The design of an informal garden, on the other hand, relies on asymmetrically placed plants, lots of curved lines, and irregular groups of plants. The hardscape may include brick or flagstone paving, a wood deck, fieldstone walls, or board-and-stake fences. Flowering perennials and rolling lawns are favorites in an informal garden. The Cottage Garden and the Cut-Flower Garden are both a happy blend of informal and formal. Each features a country-style picket fence but also has a fairly symmetrical flower garden. The curved lawn of the Cottage Garden leads from the fenced-in garden and stone patio to a border of flowering ground cover and perennials backed by evergreens. The straight lines of the stepping-stone path of the Cut-Flower Garden looks crisp and precise, but the drifts of flowers and shrubs soften any harshness.

ROSE GARDENING

Roses aren't difficult to grow if you give them the proper growing conditions. They need full sun—at least six hours a day, but more is definitely better—and good air circulation. Heavy feeders, roses need fertilizing about once a month during the growing season. They have relatively shallow roots, so they don't do well when densely planted with other plants in the same bed. That's why there should be a respectable distance of 2 to 3 feet between rose plants. Roses are ideally suited to row planting in a formal setting, and a low, clipped evergreen hedge is traditionally used to camouflage their leggy stems. The hedge also beautifies the garden without impeding air flow or competing with the roses for water and nutrients.

Although some roses are called ramblers or climbers, they aren't true vines and can't hold their own long canes vertically without help. A wooden rose arbor makes an ideal support if you lightly tie the canes with twine, allowing them to sprawl across the top of the arbor. You don't have to grow only one variety of rose along a long arbor—it may be more interesting to have several different climbers. For symmetry's sake, be sure to plant the same variety to climb up both sides of each arch.

FLOWERS FOR CUTTING

Most flower gardeners enjoy having flowers indoors as much as outdoors. You can cut flowers from any of the gardens shown in the following plans to make indoor arrangements. Remember, however, that if you bring in armloads of flowers you won't have much of a display in the garden. You may want to plant a cut-flower garden—a garden designed especially for growing flowers to harvest for indoor bouquets.

A cutting garden focuses on flowers that look beautiful and last well when they're cut for arrangements. Usually a cut-flower garden isn't for viewing because it may often be all but devoid of open blossoms, which have been cut for indoor display. Designers tuck cut-flower gardens out of the way or hide them with fencing or taller plants, as is done in the plan on page 96. Arrange the flowers within the garden in efficient rows rather than in groups or drifts, so they can be easily watered, fertilized, staked, weeded, and cut. Don't be concerned about creating an aesthetic planting scheme— colors and heights may jumble together because a cut-flower garden is, in effect, a flower-producing plot. You may wish, however, to consider the colors, shapes, and sizes of the flowers you grow so they'll combine well in a vase and harmonize with the decor of your home.

Whether your heart's dream is a formal rose garden or a quaint cottage garden, you can combine your flower gardening hobby into a livable backyard for all to admire. The following plans ought to inspire you toward greater beauty in your own backyard. And if you choose to order a plan, it will come complete with a plant list suited for your region.

Cottage Garden

The English cottage garden, beloved for its romantic, old-fashioned, homey appeal, is the kind of country garden to have again these days — whether or not you actually live in a cottage. The backyard design pictured here includes a cottage garden of easy-care, mixed perennials enclosed by a quaint picket fence. Suitable for many types of homes, from cottage to Colonial, this garden offers intimate scale and small spaces to create a comfortable backyard in which family and friends can feel at home. And there are plenty of flowers to cut all summer long for making indoor arrangements.

Paving stones lead from the front of the house to the backyard, where an arbor beckons visitors into the cozy patio and garden. Straight ahead, in the midst of the flower garden, a sundial acts as a focal point, drawing the eye right across the patio and into the garden beyond. A picket fence encloses the informal patio and flower garden, while defining the patchwork quilt of flowers inside it. Walk through the garden gate and down the path, and you will discover a garden swing nestled in the shade — a perfect spot for a romantic interlude or for whiling away the hours on a lazy afternoon.

Not to be outdone by the garden itself, the shrub borders edging the property offer an ever-changing arrangement of flowering shrubs backed by a privacy screen of tall evergreens. The trees located at each corner of the house balance and unify the patio and flower garden, while framing the garden when viewed from a distance.

Regionalized Plant Lists

Because climate and growing conditions vary greatly throughout North America, it is impossible to list here all the plants for this landscape plan that would do well everywhere on the continent. However, you can order a Blueprint Package with plant lists keyed to this plan and selected by expert horticulturists to thrive in your area.

The six-page Blueprint Package features a large-size version of this Plan View, plus a detailed regional Plant and Materials List. It also includes an illustrated list of hundreds of landscape plants suited to your region, in case you wish to make substitutions, as well as planting instructions and plant adaptation maps to ensure professional results with your new landscape.

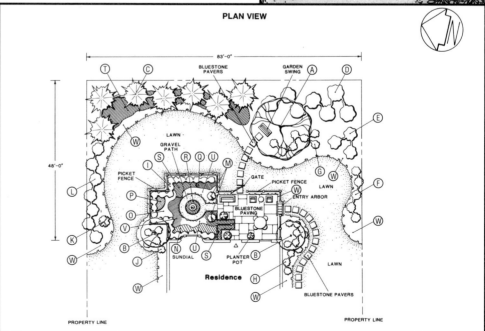

PLAN VIEW

See page 157 to order your regionalized Blueprint Package.

Landscape Plan L250 shown in summer
Designed by Michael J. Opisso

88

It isn't necessary to live in a cottage to have a cottage garden. Almost any informal home would be enhanced by this charming backyard with its effervescent color, secluded retreats, and cozy spaces — all wrapped up in a white picket fence.

Raised Perennial Border

The yard and garden pictured here would delight any flower lover, since they are designed to bloom from early spring into fall. During spring, flowering trees and shrubs, which border part of the property, provide seasonal color. The main feature of the property, however, is a dramatic perennial border designed to bloom from summer through fall. The key to creating a successful display of flowering perennials lies in choosing and combining a selection of plants that bloom together and in sequence, so the garden is never bare of flowers. When so orchestrated — as this one is — the border displays a fascinating, ever-changing collection of colors. The perennials grow in large drifts to create the most impact when viewed from across the lawn.

The planting beds surround an irregular, bow-shaped lawn, a pretty way to add interest to an uninspiring squared-off property. A low stone wall raises the planting beds several steps up, bringing the flowers closer to eye level and emphasizing the contours of the design. The low retaining wall also provides an attractive way to deal with a sloping property so the lawn can be level. If your property is flat, the wall can be eliminated without altering the basic design. Behind the perennial garden, evergreens form a background that sets off the colors in summer.

When sitting on the patio of this beautiful yard, the eye is drawn toward the gazebo, which is located two steps up from the lawn. Accessible by a stepping-stone walk, the gazebo makes a wonderful place to sit and relax in the shade while enjoying the beauty of the perennials from a different perspective.

Regionalized Plant Lists

Because climate and growing conditions vary greatly throughout North America, it is impossible to list here all the plants for this landscape plan that would do well everywhere on the continent. However, you can order a Blueprint Package with plant lists keyed to this plan and selected by expert horticulturists to thrive in your area.

The six-page Blueprint Package features a large-size version of this Plan View, plus a detailed regional Plant and Materials List. It also includes an illustrated list of hundreds of landscape plants suited to your region, in case you wish to make substitutions, as well as planting instructions and plant adaptation maps to ensure professional results with your new landscape.

See page 157 to order your regionalized Blueprint Package.

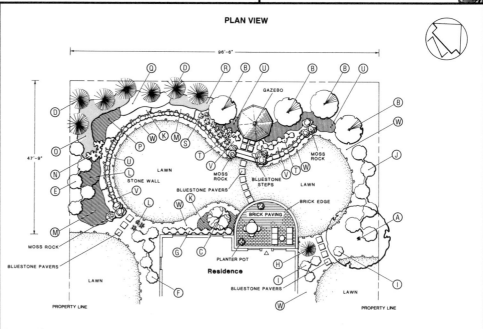

PLAN VIEW

Landscape Plan L251 shown in summer
Designed by Michael J. Opisso

Here is a yard that is alive with flowers from spring through fall. In winter, the pretty stone wall, shrubs and evergreen trees and ground covers keep the yard looking bright and beautiful.

Formal Rose Garden

The grandeur of a European palace or estate garden comes alive in the formality and scale of this landscape design, which features a formal rose garden. In creating this mood, the designer makes the landscape completely symmetrical. Both sides of the garden are exact mirror images of each other, with extensive lawn areas on each side that can be used for relaxing or entertaining.

In the tradition of the formal rose garden, neat crisp evergreen hedges outline the rose plantings, providing interest and structure even during the off-season when the roses have been cut back to near the ground. The straight lines of the stepping-stone paths form a strong cross shape in the center of the garden. Each arm of the cross begins with a formal tree rose and ends at the edge of the garden in a strong focal point. The sight line looking up the horizontal arms, which is emphasized by the overhead trellises and pergolas, terminates in groups of oval-shaped trees backed by lattice panels. Flowering vines adorn the trellises.

From the bluestone paving at the house, a sight line leads along the paving stones, past the sundial in the center of the rose garden, and culminates with a reflecting pool situated in a paved area at the far end. Note that, although the same paving material was used in the front and back areas, the pattern is formal near the house and more informal at the back. Within the strong geometrical space of the rose garden, an early-spring flowering perennial provides a blanket of color until the roses burst into their summer-long show. The rose arbor and gate at each side of the house feature climbing roses, echoing the main theme of the garden.

Regionalized Plant Lists

Because climate and growing conditions vary greatly throughout North America, it is impossible to list here all the plants for this landscape plan that would do well everywhere on the continent. However, you can order a Blueprint Package with plant lists keyed to this plan and selected by expert horticulturists to thrive in your area.

The six-page Blueprint Package features a large-size version of this Plan View, plus a detailed regional Plant and Materials List. It also includes an illustrated list of hundreds of landscape plants suited to your region, in case you wish to make substitutions, as well as planting instructions and plant adaptation maps to ensure professional results with your new landscape.

See page 157 to order your regionalized Blueprint Package.

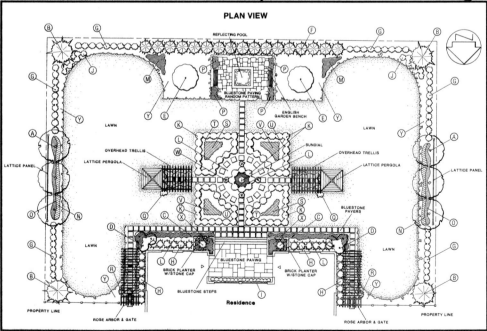

Landscape Plan L254 shown in summer
Designed by Jim Morgan

92

Here is a formal rose garden for relaxing, entertaining, or just enjoying the scent of nature's most beloved flower. Strong in line and impact, the garden is softened with overhead flowering vines and rose arbors, which provide enticing views in all directions.

Fragrance Garden

The single intention of the backyard design shown here is to provide plenty of beautiful, fragrant flowers, spring through fall, for you to gaze upon, bury your nose in, and tend with loving care. This is a gardener's garden—a garden for plant lovers.

The island bed of fragrant flowers situated off-center in the lawn balances the visual weight of the shade tree. Here, where the plants will be easily accessible from all sides, grow old-fashioned perennial bloomers whose sweet perfume has pleased generations. A weeping evergreen shrub anchors this bed, giving it year-round structure so that it looks attractive even in winter.

More fragrant perennials, planted in masses in the borders to intensify their scent, thrive in the light shade cast by the trees. Spring- and fall-blooming vines drape over the fence, softening its facade with colorful blooms. Even in early spring, fragrant-flowered bulbs push their way through the low ground cover, making perfect candidates for indoor arrangements.

The hardscape, consisting primarily of a brick patio coupled with a flagstone path leading from the gate to the patio, offers simple, yet attractive, lines. The very straightforwardness of these construction features places more importance on the garden's lovely flowers and plants. The dominant tree of the garden, a large deciduous shade tree, draws the eye to the spacious corner bed. The other trees specified are medium-sized flowering trees and evergreens for year-round greenery, while charming shrubs provide additional seasonal color.

Regionalized Plant Lists

Because climate and growing conditions vary greatly throughout North America, it is impossible to list here all the plants for this landscape plan that would do well everywhere on the continent. However, you can order a Blueprint Package with plant lists keyed to this plan and selected by expert horticulturists to thrive in your area.

The six-page Blueprint Package features a large-size version of this Plan View, plus a detailed regional Plant and Materials List. It also includes an illustrated list of hundreds of landscape plants suited to your region, in case you wish to make substitutions, as well as planting instructions and plant adaptation maps to ensure professional results with your new landscape.

See page 157 to order your regionalized Blueprint Package.

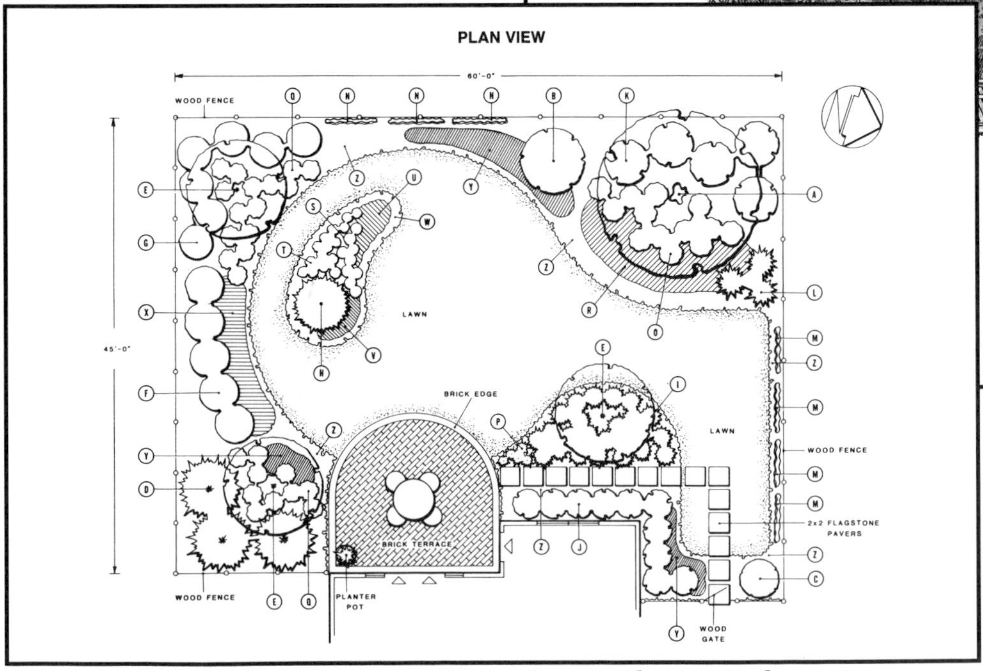

PLAN VIEW

Landscape Plan L269 shown in summer
Designed by Damon Scott

94

If you're a flower lover, this backyard plan filled with fragrant flowers is for you. The teardrop-shaped island bed, planted with a collection of scented perennials, is designed so you can enjoy the plants close up and tend them from all sides. The elegant brick patio, shaped to mirror the planting bed to its right, provides ample space for the family to dine and relax.

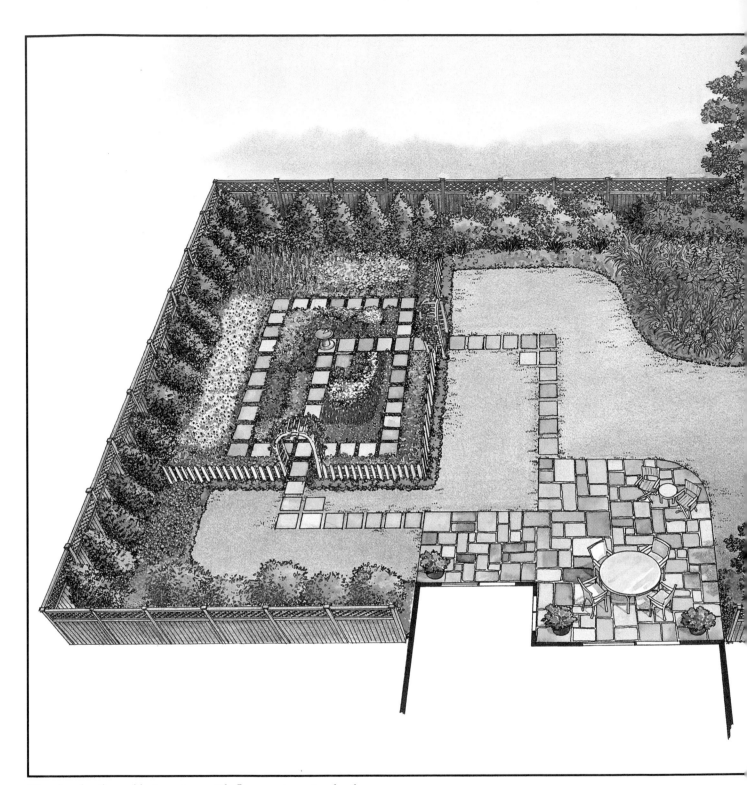

Here's a backyard brimming with flowers to enjoy both indoors and outdoors. You can harvest armloads of flowers from the gated cut-flower garden to display in your home and admire the blooming landscape from the vantage point of the roomy flagstone patio.

Cut-Flower Garden

Y ou can have your garden flowers and cut them too with this charming backyard plan. The designer skillfully created a landscape that features a garden planted just to produce flowers to cut for indoor arrangements, yet still looks as pretty as a picture. Here you'll find a serious gardening plot attractively integrated into a landscape of flowering trees, shrubs, and ground covers with plenty of patio and lawn for the family.

Because you'll be removing most of the flowers as they begin to open, a cut-flower garden has more in common with a vegetable garden than a flower garden, so it's best to camouflage the plants from direct view. The designer chose a white picket fence to surround the garden, hiding the beds and providing an attractive year-round structure. Two gated arbors, draped with flowering vines, provide easy access to the garden. The flowers planted in front of the fence aren't meant for cutting but for you to enjoy while relaxing on the patio.

Within the gated cut-flower garden itself, stepping-stone paths provide easy access for tending the flower beds. The designer devoted one section to perennial flowers, which return to grace the garden year after year. Another section contains annuals, which need replanting each year. The perennials include an assortment of spring-, summer-, and fall-blooming plants so you'll have months of different blossoms to cut, while the long-blooming annuals keep on producing more flowers after they're cut. All the flowers specified for this design make long-lasting arrangements.

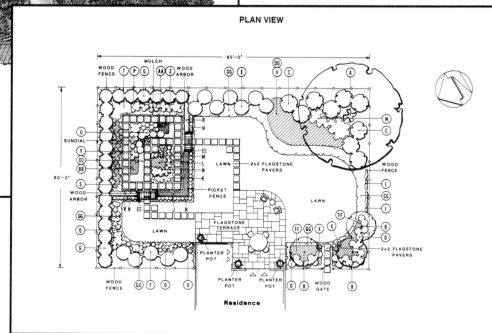

Landscape Plan L270 shown in summer
Designed by Damon Scott

Regionalized Plant Lists

Because climate and growing conditions vary greatly throughout North America, it is impossible to list here all the plants for this landscape plan that would do well everywhere on the continent. However, you can order a Blueprint Package with plant lists keyed to this plan and selected by expert horticulturists to thrive in your area.

The six-page Blueprint Package features a large-size version of this Plan View, plus a detailed regional Plant and Materials List. It also includes an illustrated list of hundreds of landscape plants suited to your region, in case you wish to make substitutions, as well as planting instructions and plant adaptation maps to ensure professional results with your new landscape.

See page 157 to order your regionalized Blueprint Package.

Garden design: Conni Cross

Located just off the dining room, a brick patio shaded by a small flowering tree offers a pleasant and convenient spot to sit and dine outdoors while enjoying the beautiful garden close at hand.

98

BACKYARDS FOR OUTDOOR LIVING

Relax in Comfort in These Very Livable "Outdoor Rooms"

The primary consideration in designing a backyard for outdoor living is to plan for comfort. You'll want a large hard surface for holding tables, chairs, and lounge furniture; privacy from the neighbors; and protection from the elements. The designs featured in this chapter were created for families wishing to optimize their use of the outdoors. Each provides plenty of area for family and guests to get together and relax while enjoying the beautifully planted garden in comfort.

A DESIGN TO SUIT YOUR LIFESTYLE

When designing a backyard with a lot of outdoor living space, first consider exactly how you want to use the space. Do you want the space primarily for family use, for entertaining, or both? Do you and your family wish to spend hours outdoors sunning and barbecuing or lounging in the shade? When entertaining, is your style a catered cocktail party or a pot-luck picnic? Do you usually entertain a few close friends, a pack of family members, or a large number of business acquaintances? Will you be using the yard primarily in the daylight hours, at night, or at all hours? After you consider exactly how you'll be using the area, you'll be better able to plan a beautiful and functional landscape.

THE MAIN OUTDOOR ROOM

Start thinking of your backyard garden as an outdoor living room and plan it accordingly. Think of the area adjacent to the house as a room that makes the transition from the indoors to the outdoors. Create a large patio or deck there to define the main outdoor living space—the area where you'll be relaxing and entertaining. You'll want easy access from the house to this outdoor living space, especially if you entertain a lot, so position this main area adjacent to doors leading from the kitchen and other rooms.

Choose a flooring material that complements the architecture of your home and your lifestyle. The choice of wood, stone, or brick for the hardscape determines the ambience you create in your backyard. Wood seems the most casual and naturalistic, whereas brick and stone look more formal and elegant. You can mix materials, creating a brick patio a step down from a wood deck, as is done effectively in Plan L240 on page 106. In addition to extending the entertaining area, the terrace provides an easy transition from the deck to the garden. The most formal design shown in this chapter, Plan L243 on page 108, makes the transition from the house to the outdoors with a flagstone patio abutting a formal brick patio with a central fountain.

If you throw a very large party, these designs offer enough room so the overflow of people from the patio or deck can easily spill onto the lawn. Unlike the indoor rooms of the house, these outdoor rooms have no walls, so people on the lawn can easily mingle and converse with those on the terrace.

Landscape design: Ireland-Gannon Associates

This flower-filled raised sitting area above the main section of the deck creates an inviting spot for relaxing in the sun while enjoying the vista beyond.

Controlling Sun and Shade

Imagine sitting down to lunch at a beautifully set table on a sunny stone terrace in July. Not very inviting, is it? Although that setting may be perfect for sunbathers, the lunch crowd would bake. All the designs in this chapter include a large deciduous shade tree or two strategically placed near the deck or patio. Because the trees are leafless in spring and late autumn and in full leaf in summer, they help create a comfortable setting. They allow warming sun to reach the patio during the seasons when the rays feel good, and they cast shade in summer when you welcome the coolness.

Anyone wishing to bask in the sun can always move out of the tree's shadow, either onto another part of the terrace or into an open area in the garden. The designs allow for plenty of open, unshaded areas to keep sun worshipers and gardeners happy. In addition to modifying the sun's effects, the trees act as a gentle windbreak, keeping the area comfort-able in the evening both early and late in the season. Notice that the designers situated the trees back into the garden area so that fallen leaves or flowers wouldn't have to be constantly cleaned up to keep the area tidy. In addition, they chose low-maintenance trees that don't constantly shed their leaves.

Outdoor Kitchens for Easy Entertaining

If you enjoy cooking outdoors and do it frequently, you'll be in your element with an outdoor living space containing a built-in barbecue, such as that featured in the Weekend Retreat. Think of the convenience of having the barbecue exactly where you need it when you need it. No more groping in the dark or dragging the barbecue out of the garage or storage shed. It's right there, just waiting to be used. The added convenience of adjoining service cabinets lets you enjoy outdoor life without constantly running back and forth to the kitchen. You can have mats, napkins, cutlery, dishes, and barbecue supplies right at your fingertips. When hosting a party, the service cabinets can double as a bar, with extra bottles stored below, and plenty of space for mixing drinks on the countertop.

CREATING A SPECIAL PLACE TO RELAX

In addition to a deck or patio large enough to accommodate family and guests, you may want to have another smaller, more intimate area where you can enjoy the backyard from a different vantage point.

Rest in a Shaded Hammock

A hammock is an ideal place for total relaxation. It can be the freestanding type supported by a metal frame or the type that hangs between two trees. Since it isn't easy to relax for any period of time in a hammock with the sun beating down on you, locate the hammock in a shady spot in the backyard. Or go one step farther. The Weekend Retreat (see Plan L271 on page 102) includes an arbor with a hammock suspended in the shelter, where you can relax and view the garden while being protected from the sun. On a hot day, you'll find it as much as 15 degrees cooler under the shade of the arbor. You can use the arbor for a romantic hideaway for two on a starlit night, as a sheltered haven for children to play or nap, or as an outdoor refuge on a rainy afternoon. Surrounded by flowers, you'll get a sense of being one with the garden when you lie in the hammock and gaze out onto the beauty that is your very own backyard.

A Gazebo for Privacy and Entertaining

A gazebo makes an attractive and functional addition to any backyard. Sheltered from the elements and enclosed by walls and a roof, it can be used for an intimate, romantic dinner for two or cocktails for eight or ten. A gazebo offers a cool spot for a family lunch on a sunny day or a protected retreat on a day when there's a light misting rain.

Since a gazebo draws the eye by its shape and size, it acts as a dramatic focal point in the garden. Choose a romantic, gingerbread-style structure for a flowery landscape or the clean lines of a more contemporary style for a simpler setting. Whichever you choose, don't just plunk it down in the yard—tie the gazebo to the landscape with a walk and attractive plantings.

PRIVACY TO ENJOY YOUR SPACE

While you enjoy your outdoor living room, you may not want to look into your neighbors' homes and yards. For that matter, you probably don't want them to see what you're up to all the time, either. You'll want the freedom to sunbathe or entertain in the privacy of your own backyard without the neighbors ogling your every movement.

The backyard plans featured in this chapter use the landscaping to attractively create the privacy you want. Strategically located evergreen trees and shrubs act as stalwart bastions of privacy the year around. They screen views while beautifying the landscape and softening the security fencing behind them.

BRIGHT IDEAS FOR NIGHTTIME LIGHTING

No doubt, you'll be using your outdoor living area in the evenings. Without a good lighting plan you'll be left totally in the dark, and that can shorten the hours you have to enjoy your garden as well as prove dangerous. With a creative lighting plan, your outdoor living area can become even more spectacular at night than it is during the day.

Observe the way the light of the sun and moon play on the landscape and then imagine duplicating the effects that please you the most. Decide what the focal point of the backyard lighting will be, choosing a walkway, deck, terrace, large tree, or other part of the landscape for dramatic lighting. More than two focal points are confusing, so limit yourself to one or two. The rest of the lighting should be softer and built around the focal point.

Basic Lighting Techniques

Using just three basic techniques, you can give a professional look to your backyard at night.

Downlighting, as the name implies, comes from above, simulating the sun or moon depending on the fixtures and the wattage of the bulbs used. This type of lighting works well as safety lighting or basic illumination for pathways, steps, and decks. Be sure to locate fixtures so they don't shine directly in your eyes.

In uplighting, the light comes from below, shining dramatically up into the area to be illuminated. Usually floodlights or spotlights are used to uplight a picturesque tree or wall. If the uplighting isn't directly vertical, but angled, it brings out intriguing textures in bark, foliage, walls, and fences. Uplighting takes on a subtle tone when low-wattage bulbs are used.

Backlighting casts indirect silhouettes and shadows created by lighting the surface behind a dark object, such as a tree or statue. A tree near the house can be backlit by angling the light to shine on the house. The reflected light effectively silhouettes the tree and provides safety lighting.

Beautifully serene when viewed from inside the house, the special landscape designs presented here beckon you to come outdoors and experience them firsthand. Your family and guests will experience all the comforts of your home while enjoying the fresh air and flowers surrounding them in these beautiful garden settings.

Weekend Retreat

This colorful backyard serves as a special weekend retreat where you and your family can spend your free time relaxing and entertaining. Enjoy a quiet afternoon reading or lounging in the hammock under the romantic arbor, or host a cookout for your friends on the spacious patio complete with an outdoor kitchen.

Both the patio and the hammock provide refuge from the hot summer sun—a vine-covered overhead trellis and leafy trees protect the patio, and the hammock hideaway (plans available separately) tucked in the corner of the yard can catch a breeze while reflecting the sun's hot rays. Just right for a lazy afternoon snooze, the hammock structure nestles within an intimate flowery setting that encloses and enhances the space. Flagstone pavers lead the way from the patio to the hammock, following the gentle curve of the border, and flagstones mark the entrance from the gates at each side of the yard for easy access.

Privacy-protecting evergreen trees and shrubs fill the rear of the property, and all are gracefully set off by a purple-foliaged weeping specimen tree located on sight lines from both the patio and the arbor. (In some regions, another type of eye-catching specimen tree is substituted for the purple-foliaged tree.) For color contrast, long-blooming, yellow-flowering perennials surround the tree. The designer included large patches of other easy-care perennials that punctuate the rest of the landscape with splashes of color from spring through fall to create a welcoming backyard retreat.

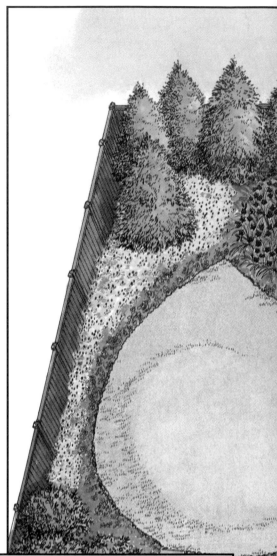

Regionalized Plant Lists

Because climate and growing conditions vary greatly throughout North America, it is impossible to list here all the plants for this landscape plan that would do well everywhere on the continent. However, you can order a Blueprint Package with plant lists keyed to this plan and selected by expert horticulturists to thrive in your area.

The six-page Blueprint Package features a large-size version of this Plan View, plus a detailed regional Plant and Materials List. It also includes an illustrated list of hundreds of landscape plants suited to your region, in case you wish to make substitutions, as well as planting instructions and plant adaptation maps to ensure professional results with your new landscape.

See page 157 to order your regionalized Blueprint Package.

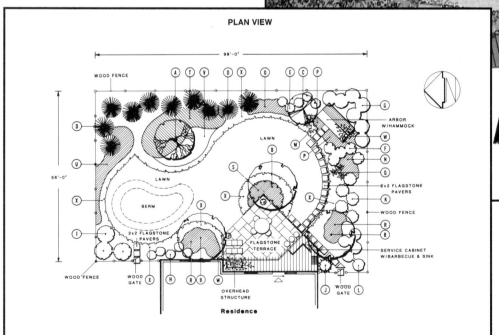

Landscape Plan L271 shown in summer
Designed by Michael J. Opisso

For hammock structure plans, see page 148.

An arbor-covered hammock and a spacious patio with a kitchen provide comfortable spots for relaxing outdoors while enjoying the colorful flowering perennials. The bermed soil on the left side of the lawn adds dimension and visually counterweights the patio, while providing a complementary curve.

Spacious Deck and Gazebo

There's something enticing—and romantic—about a garden gazebo. It creates an intimate spot to sit and talk, perhaps making the difference between having a few friends over and having a party. If you enjoy entertaining, this backyard design featuring both a roomy deck and a lovely gazebo may be the one for your family.

The gazebo (plans available separately) acts as the main focal point of the design, drawing the eye by its shape, size, and location and enticing visitors by the stepping-stone path leading to its cozy confines. The lush plantings surrounding the gazebo anchor it to the design, creating a flowery setting that helps keep the structure cool and inviting.

The other primary feature of this garden is a large deck (plans available separately). The deck features octagonal lines to echo and complement the shape of the gazebo and has enough room to accommodate two separate dining tables. On the practical side, a built-in barbecue and a storage cabinet turn the deck into an outdoor extension of your home's living space.

The informal style of the design incorporates sunny and shady areas, as well as a mix of evergreen and deciduous trees and shrubs, to create a variety of textures and patterns. Background plantings of tall evergreens assure privacy, and a wide variety of flowering shrubs and perennials add seasonal color and interest. Three deciduous shade trees frame the skyline, provide necessary summer shade, and let in warming winter sun.

Regionalized Plant Lists

Because climate and growing conditions vary greatly throughout North America, it is impossible to list here all the plants for this landscape plan that would do well everywhere on the continent. However, you can order a Blueprint Package with plant lists keyed to this plan and selected by expert horticulturists to thrive in your area.

The six-page Blueprint Package features a large-size version of this Plan View, plus a detailed regional Plant and Materials List. It also includes an illustrated list of hundreds of landscape plants suited to your region, in case you wish to make substitutions, as well as planting instructions and plant adaptation maps to ensure professional results with your new landscape.

See page 157 to order your regionalized Blueprint Package.

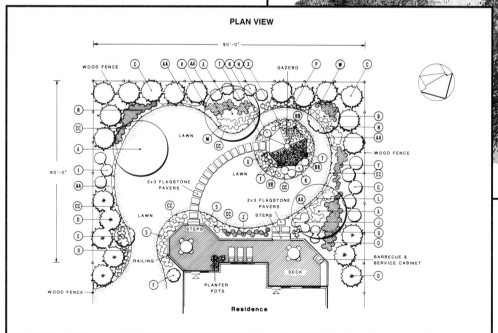

Landscape Plan L272 shown in summer
Designed by David Poplawski

For Deck Plan D119, see page 153.
For gazebo plans, see page 148.

If you enjoy entertaining, this backyard plan is bound to please you. Designed for fun and romance, the visual interest and action revolve around the gazebo. It's balanced by a spacious deck, three deciduous shade trees, and deep planting borders featuring colorful flowering shrubs and perennials. The curving shape of the lawn unifies the design.

Designed for families who love outdoor living, this backyard features a deck and patio combination that is perfect for entertaining. It features separate areas for cooking and dining, intimate conversations, and relaxing in the sun.

Deck and Terrace for Entertaining

The perfect setting for an outdoor party — or for simply relaxing with family and friends — this backyard features an elegant wooden deck and brick patio that run the length of the house. The deck area on the right acts as an outdoor kitchen, featuring a built-in barbecue, serving cabinet, and space enough for a dining table and chairs. For those who opt to mingle with the other guests, rather than kibitz with the cook, a separate area has been provided at the other end.

Built at the same level as the house, and easily accessible from inside, the deck extends the interior living space to the outdoors. Three lovely flowering trees shade the deck and house, while creating a visual ceiling and walls to reinforce further the idea that these areas are outdoor rooms.

Down a few steps from the deck, the brick terrace makes a transition between the house (and deck) and the garden. Open on two sides to the lawn, this sunny terrace feels — and is — spacious and open, creating a great place in which people can mingle and talk during a cocktail party or sunbathe on a Saturday afternoon. From here, it's possible to enjoy the garden setting close at hand. The plantings around the perimeter of the yard feature several kinds of tall evergreens to provide privacy. In front of the evergreens, large drifts of flowering perennials are perfectly displayed against the green background. Between the evergreens, masses of shrubbery provide a changing color show from early spring through fall.

PLAN VIEW

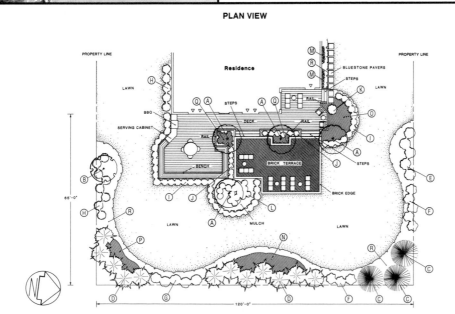

Landscape Plan L240 shown in spring
Designed by Michael J. Opisso

Regionalized Plant Lists

Because climate and growing conditions vary greatly throughout North America, it is impossible to list here all the plants for this landscape plan that would do well everywhere on the continent. However, you can order a Blueprint Package with plant lists keyed to this plan and selected by expert horticulturists to thrive in your area.

The six-page Blueprint Package features a large-size version of this Plan View, plus a detailed regional Plant and Materials List. It also includes an illustrated list of hundreds of landscape plants suited to your region, in case you wish to make substitutions, as well as planting instructions and plant adaptation maps to ensure professional results with your new landscape.

See page 157 to order your regionalized Blueprint Package.

Formal Garden for Entertaining

Want to play a role from the Great Gatsby? Then close your eyes and imagine being a guest at a large party in this magnificent garden designed for formal entertaining. Imagine standing in the house at the French doors, just at the entrance to the paved area, and looking out at this perfectly symmetrical scene. The left mirrors the right; a major sight line runs straight down the center past the fountain to the statue that serves as a focal point at the rear of the garden. Three perfectly oval flowing trees on each side of the patio frame the sight line, as well as help to delineate the pavement from the planted areas of the garden.

The flagstone patio along the house rises several steps above the brick patio, giving it prominence and presenting a good view of the rest of the property. The change in paving materials provides a separate identity to each area, yet by edging the brick with bluestone to match the upper patio, the two are tied together.

Pink and purple flowering shrubs and perennials provide an elegant color scheme throughout the growing season. A vine-covered lattice panel, featuring royal purple flowers that bloom all summer long, creates a secluded area accessible by paving stones at the rear of the property. What a perfect spot for a romantic rendezvous!

Regionalized Plant Lists

Because climate and growing conditions vary greatly throughout North America, it is impossible to list here all the plants for this landscape plan that would do well everywhere on the continent. However, you can order a Blueprint Package with plant lists keyed to this plan and selected by expert horticulturists to thrive in your area.

The six-page Blueprint Package features a large-size version of this Plan View, plus a detailed regional Plant and Materials List. It also includes an illustrated list of hundreds of landscape plants suited to your region, in case you wish to make substitutions, as well as planting instructions and plant adaptation maps to ensure professional results with your new landscape.

See page 157 to order your regionalized Blueprint Package.

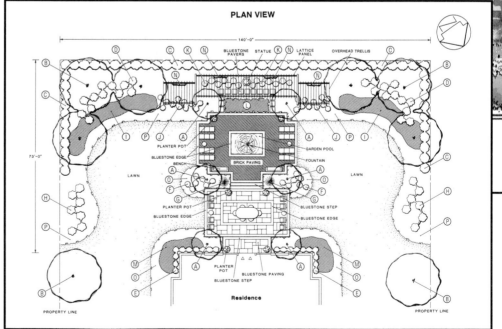

Landscape Plan L243 shown in summer
Designed by Michael J. Opisso

108

This formal garden provides a perfect setting for romantic outdoor parties or for simply relaxing in the sun on a Saturday afternoon.

High above the rest of the garden, this second-story deck affords a beautiful view of the grounds. And the deck looks beautiful too, because latticework and soft plantings integrate it into the landscape.

Second-Story Deck

A second-story deck can be the answer to many different land-scaping problems. Sometimes it is built at a mother-daughter house to provide a private deck for a second-story apartment. Where a house is built on sloping property, which cannot accommodate a ground-level deck, a raised deck is the answer. With split-level or raised-ranch houses, where the kitchen is often on the second level, a second-story deck right off the kitchen eliminates carrying food and dishes up and down stairs.

Even though a deck is high, it can have two levels and therefore two separate use areas, as the designer accomplishes with this deck. The upper area features a built-in barbecue, service cabinet, and space for dining. The lower area invites family and guests to lounge and relax in the sun. Because the deck is high enough off the ground that an accidental fall could be dangerous, a railing and planters that double as a railing ensure safety. Filled with masses of annuals, the planters bring living color above ground.

Without screening, the underside of the deck would be an eyesore when viewed from the yard. The designer solved this problem by enclosing the void beneath the deck with latticework and using a hedge to soften the effect. If the area beneath the deck is to be used as storage, a door can be added to the latticework. The triangular shape of the deck is far more pleasing than a square or rectangular design. Three flowering trees at the corners of the deck anchor this triangular shape and further serve to bring color and greenery up high. Tall evergreens help to screen the deck from the neighbors.

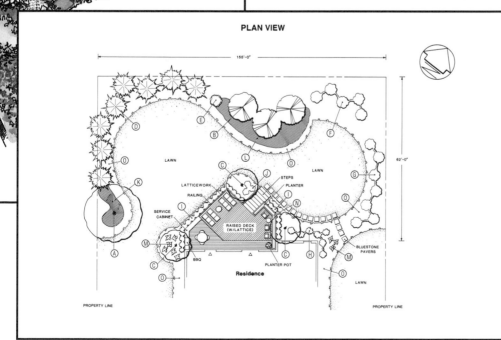

Landscape Plan L249 shown in summer
Designed by Michael J. Opisso

Regionalized Plant Lists

Because climate and growing conditions vary greatly throughout North America, it is impossible to list here all the plants for this landscape plan that would do well everywhere on the continent. However, you can order a Blueprint Package with plant lists keyed to this plan and selected by expert horticulturists to thrive in your area.

The six-page Blueprint Package features a large-size version of this Plan View, plus a detailed regional Plant and Materials List. It also includes an illustrated list of hundreds of landscape plants suited to your region, in case you wish to make substitutions, as well as planting instructions and plant adaptation maps to ensure professional results with your new landscape.

See page 157 to order your regionalized Blueprint Package.

Set off by a lush planting of ornamental grasses, this garden pool and waterfall lure birds and small animals into the yard to quench their thirst.

BACKYARDS TO ATTRACT WILDLIFE

Specially Designed Gardens Offer Food, Water, and Shelter to Birds and Butterflies

Any garden is a joy to behold, but a garden designed especially to attract wildlife includes the added beauty and excitement of birds, butterflies, and small animals that come to visit or set up residence. With their colorful plumage, amusing antics, and lyrical songs, birds provide entertainment for the whole family. You and your children will find bird watching a pleasant diversion that can develop into a lifelong hobby. Children find hummingbirds, with their hovering flight and darting speed, and butterflies, with their patterned wings and graceful flight, especially delightful.

ESSENTIALS OF A WILDLIFE GARDEN

In creating a garden to attract wildlife—whether you're attracting birds, butterflies, chipmunks, or squirrels—you must plan to meet their year-round needs for food, water, and shelter. A variety of plants can offer food and sanctuary for desirable species of wildlife while transforming your yard into a beautiful showplace that invites family and friends to stop and rest.

Think twice before applying any herbicides or other pesticides in a wildlife garden. The weed or insect that you just sprayed may become food for a bird or other animal higher on the food chain and may very well prove toxic to the creature that eats it.

Feeders and Natural Food Sources

You can attract wildlife simply by putting out food in feeders or scattering it on the ground. In the long run, it's much more economical, and certainly more natural, to grow plants that provide a source of berries, nuts, and nectar for birds, butterflies, and animals to eat. Of course, the wildlife planting can double as an ornamental landscape planting, as the plans in this chapter demonstrate, so you can have your garden and the wildlife, too.

Providing Food for Songbirds

Have you ever noticed the happy, and sometimes frenzied, activity surrounding a bird feeder? Chickadees and finches perch at the feeder to eat, while cardinals and mourning doves feast on seeds that fall to the ground. Look around and you'll see other birds and creatures jockeying for position. Blue jays hover in the air, awaiting an opportunity to nudge their way onto the perch; goldfinches politely wait in nearby trees and shrubs, taking turns with those at the feeder.

Even in the most naturalistic garden, locating several types of feeders close to the house allows for good bird watching the year around. Washing dishes and preparing meals becomes a pleasant task if you can look out the kitchen window and watch your feathered friends enjoying a meal at a nearby feeder. Feeders can be simple or elaborate, store-bought or homemade, depending on your taste and budget. (For plans for several decorative bird feeders, see page 149.)

Different types of seeds appeal to different birds, but if you've ever hung a bird feeder, you know that squirrels will pilfer any type of birdseed. Squirrel-proof bird feeders, especially those approved by the Audubon Society, work well to keep squirrels from raiding the bird food. You may also wish to scatter cracked corn on the ground for the squirrels and chipmunks to distract them from the more expensive birdseed.

In addition to furnishing shelter and nesting sites, the shrubs and trees in your garden should also provide a source of fruit, nuts, and berries for the birds and squirrels. These special plantings will attract lots of birds to your garden. Choose plants for continuous bloom throughout spring and summer, so the fruit, nuts, and seeds will ripen and provide a food source beginning in summer and lasting through the winter. Most birds, even those that eat seeds from a feeder, also devour an enormous number of insects — another good reason to attract feathered friends to your yard.

Providing Food for Hummingbirds

Anyone who has seen a hummingbird feeder with its red-tinted sugar water knows that hummingbirds find red an irresistible color. Since hummingbirds associate red with food, they'll investigate anything that color, whether it's a red flower or a red bandanna hanging on the wash line to dry. The best flowers for attracting hummingbirds are pink, red, or orange nectar-bearing blossoms with a tubular shape to accommodate their long beaks. The Hummingbird Garden (L274 on page 120) relies on plants specially selected to provide nectar to keep the hummingbirds well nourished from spring through fall.

Hummingbirds are very territorial and will do their utmost to keep others out of their feeding area. Not only will a hummingbird challenge another hummer, it may even try to chase off butterflies, other small birds, and even small animals such as chipmunks with much noise and a fluttering of wings. Because they're so territorial, you may find it necessary to create separate plantings throughout your yard in order to attract more than one hummingbird pair.

Providing Food for Butterflies

When considering gardening for butterflies, most people tend to forget the less attractive — and sometimes destructive — caterpillar stage that butterflies

Butterflies flock to nectar-rich blossoms, such as this rubrum lily, and can be invited into a garden by planting quantities of their favorite flowers.

go through before they metamorphose into the colorful winged creatures we enjoy. Instead of spurning all caterpillars in the garden, you must learn to differentiate between "good bugs" and "bad bugs" to enjoy an abundance of butterflies. Knowing that the caterpillar eating its way through the foliage of your parsley, dill, and carrots will grow up to become a gorgeous black swallowtail butterfly helps you to look more favorably on it. Perhaps you'll plant enough parsley to feed both yourself and the caterpillars so that later you can enjoy both herbs and butterflies.

Learn which butterflies are native to your locale and which migrate through it so you can identify them in the adult butterfly stage and, more importantly, in the caterpillar stage. You'll still want to pick off destructive caterpillars, such as the tomato hornworm and the cabbage white butterfly, while nurturing those caterpillars that will later spin cocoons and hatch into charming butterflies.

Thirst-Quenching Water

Wildlife of all kinds will gratefully frequent your yard if it offers a source of water for drinking or bathing. The water source may be as simple as a birdbath or as elaborate as a garden pond, but keep in mind that the greater the water surface, the larger and more varied the species of wildlife that will be attracted into the garden. Depending on its size and depth, a pond can attract everything from songbirds to ducks, and chipmunks to deer. Larger birds, such as ducks and geese, find bigger ponds attractive.

Before stocking a garden pool with fish, be aware of the wildlife in your area and learn about their feeding habits. You may be greatly distressed to stock a pond with glimmering koi only to have some hungry heron or ravenous racoon make a dinner of the expensive fish. Even goldfish sometimes furnish a good meal for cats or wild animals, so you may need to put up a barrier around your yard to keep the predatory animals away from the pond.

Besides providing thirst-quenching water for the critters, a garden pool becomes a lovely focal point, adding greatly to the garden scenery. A pond is easily installed by do-it-yourselfers using a PVC liner or a preformed fiberglass pond liner, both of which are available in many sizes and shapes. A landscape contractor can also install the pond for you. A good reference book for do-it-yourselfers is Ortho's *Garden Pools and Fountains*, which describes how to keep a small pool ecologically balanced and mosquito free.

If a pond isn't for you, a birdbath will suffice as a wildlife water source. You'll be delighted with the variety of songbirds it can attract. A permanent plastic-lined puddle, bordered by low flat rocks, provides a perfect water source for hummingbirds and butterflies. Puddles and ponds also attract toads and frogs, which are among nature's best insect eaters. They, along with fish, help keep a still pond free of mosquitoes.

In the garden plans presented in this chapter, notice that the designer located the water in partially open areas. The water shouldn't be totally hidden from view, or you won't be able to watch the critters that come to drink and bathe. Some shelter should be provided, however, since the birds and animals will feel safer with nearby hiding places. Trees and shrubs provide convenient perches for birds waiting their turn at the water, and they offer an escape from predators.

Creating Shelter and Cover

Birds and other wildlife need shelter as protection from predators and the elements, as well as a place to build their nests. A variety of shelters—both natural and constructed—provides wildlife with places to make permanent homes. Both evergreen and deciduous trees are ideal for many types of nesting birds, but some birds prefer sites closer to or on the ground, with dense shrubs and thickets providing the right environment. In cold climates, evergreens make especially good shelters during winter storms. The plans on pages 118 and 120 offer dense plantings suitable for sheltering birds.

A birdhouse in your landscape will offer a ready-to-move-in abode to a nesting pair, which may return to your yard regularly from then on. You can make your own or buy simple or elaborate ones, ranging from a single-holed nesting box to a high rise for purple martins. You may even wish to build a birdhouse that's a scaled-down replica of your own house for a clever addition to the garden. (See plans for decorative birdhouses on page 149.)

Choose a picnic or patio table or an open spot on the deck or near the lawn to leave nest-building materials for birds in the springtime. Put out bits of string, twine, small twigs, and even lint from your clothes dryer, and you'll find birds making themselves at home in your yard.

Butterflies are cold-blooded and love to spread their wings in the sunshine, soaking up the sun's warmth. Flat rocks in a sunny spot, ideally located near water, will attract them in droves. Create this spot where it's also sheltered from the wind, so the insects can hunker down during a rainstorm and their wings won't be windblown.

When you design a wildlife garden, most of your efforts go into creating the habitat for the wildlife—but don't forget a habitat for yourself, as shown in the plans that follow. A deck extending into the garden offers a perfect place for bird and animal watching. Comfortable seating in a woodland or meadow or near a birdbath or pond allows you to watch quietly and enjoy the beauty you've created and the wildlife you've invited to share it.

Landscape design: Audrey Bruce

Birds and other wildlife may find water scarcer than food, so if you want to attract them to your garden it's a good idea to provide a source of water. A garden pool like this one not only creates a pretty focal point in the landscape, it provides drinking water for a variety of animals.

The abundant flowers in this backyard turn it into a paradise for butterflies as well as for garden lovers. Dozens of different kinds of nectar-rich plants, blooming from spring through fall, provide the necessary blossoms to lure the ephemeral beauties not only to stop and pay a visit, but perhaps to stay and set up a home.

Butterfly Garden

Colorful butterflies will flock to this floriferous backyard, which is planted with flowering shrubs and perennials irresistible to these welcome winged visitors. A butterfly's needs are simple: a sunny spot out of the wind to perch on, a puddle of water to drink from, nectar-rich flowers to sip from, and food plants for the caterpillar phase to munch on. The designer incorporated all these needs into this landscape plan, while also providing for human visitors.

The flagstone patio, nestled among the flowers near the center of the yard, brings you away from the house right out where the butterflies congregate. This is a perfect place for a table and chairs, where you can sip coffee during a sunny spring morning or dine during a summer evening, all the while keeping an eye out for a visiting monarch, red admiral, or swallowtail feeding on the nearby flowers or perching on the flat rocks near the puddle. The wood swing and arbor (plans available separately), located on the far right, provide a cool spot to relax as you while away the hours admiring the garden and its beautiful butterfly guests.

Instead of a pure grass lawn, the designer specified a lawn composed of mixed clover and grass. The clover provides nectar for the adult butterflies and forage for the caterpillars. Keep in mind that, as beautiful as they are, butterflies are insects. To enjoy the elusive winged stage, you'll have to tolerate a little feeding damage from the caterpillar stage. It's best to garden organically, steering clear of all insecticides — whether chemical or biological — in this garden, or you're likely to have few butterfly visitors.

Regionalized Plant Lists

Because climate and growing conditions vary greatly throughout North America, it is impossible to list here all the plants for this landscape plan that would do well everywhere on the continent. However, you can order a Blueprint Package with plant lists keyed to this plan and selected by expert horticulturists to thrive in your area.

The six-page Blueprint Package features a large-size version of this Plan View, plus a detailed regional Plant and Materials List. It also includes an illustrated list of hundreds of landscape plants suited to your region, in case you wish to make substitutions, as well as planting instructions and plant adaptation maps to ensure professional results with your new landscape.

See page 157 to order your regionalized Blueprint Package.

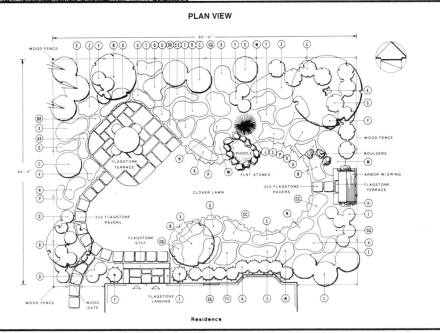

PLAN VIEW

Landscape Plan L273 shown in summer
Designed by Tom Nordloh

For swing and arbor plans, see page 149.

Nature lovers will delight in the abundant birds that will flock to this beautiful garden. An attractive collection of berried plants and evergreens offers food and shelter for the wildlife, while creating a handsome, pastoral setting.

Garden to Attract Birds

There is no better way to wake up in the morning than to the sound of songbirds in the garden. Wherever you live, you will be surprised at the number and variety of birds you can attract by offering them a few basic necessities — water, shelter, nesting spots, and food. Birds need water for drinking and bathing. They need shrubs and trees, especially evergreens, for shelter and nesting. Edge spaces — open areas with trees nearby for quick protection — provide ground feeders with foraging places, while plants with berries and nuts offer other natural sources of food.

The garden presented here contains all the necessary elements to attract birds to the garden. The shrubs and trees are chosen especially to provide a mix of evergreen and deciduous species. All of these, together with the masses of flowering perennials, bear seeds, nuts or berries known to appeal to birds. The berry show looks quite pretty, too, until the birds gobble them up. Planted densely enough for necessary shelter, the bird-attracting plants create a backyard that's enjoyable throughout the seasons.

The birdbath is located in the lawn so it will be in the sun. A naturalistic pond provides water in a more protected setting. The birdhouses and feeders aren't necessary — though they may be the icing on the cake when it comes to luring the largest number of birds — because the landscape provides abundant natural food and shelter. Outside one of the main windows of the house, a birdfeeder hangs from a small flowering tree, providing up-close viewing of your feathered friends.

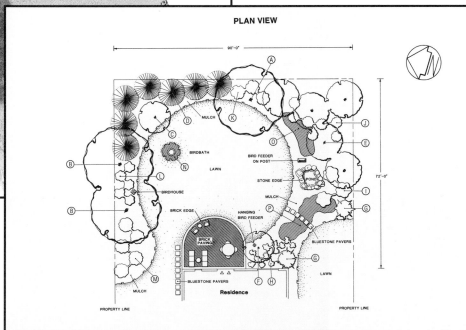

PLAN VIEW

Landscape Plan L245 shown in autumn
Designed by Michael J. Opisso

Regionalized Plant Lists

Because climate and growing conditions vary greatly throughout North America, it is impossible to list here all the plants for this landscape plan that would do well everywhere on the continent. However, you can order a Blueprint Package with plant lists keyed to this plan and selected by expert horticulturists to thrive in your area.

The six-page Blueprint Package features a large-size version of this Plan View, plus a detailed regional Plant and Materials List. It also includes an illustrated list of hundreds of landscape plants suited to your region, in case you wish to make substitutions, as well as planting instructions and plant adaptation maps to ensure professional results with your new landscape.

See page 157 to order your regionalized Blueprint Package.

119

Hummingbird Garden

Quick as lightning and jealous of "their" garden, hummingbirds provide exciting backyard entertainment and are easy to attract with the right plantings. Although many people supply them with a sugar-and-water feeder, hummingbirds need vitamin-rich flower nectar for complete nourishment. Hummingbirds love red. They busily investigate all red flowers—and even red objects bearing little resemblance to flowers—preferring trumpet-shaped types accommodating their long beaks. To thrive in a garden, hummingbirds also need a source of water.

The designer created this backyard plan as a charming informal setting to attract hummingbirds from spring through fall, while arranging colors and plant textures to make a visual picture that will please you and your family throughout the year. The birdbath, surrounded by some of the hummers' favorite annual flowers, punctuates the circular lawn area. Just beyond, a wood swing suspended from a cozy arbor (plans available separately) provides the perfect spot for bird watching. Evergreen shrubs and tall shade trees provide nesting sites and, at the same time, enclose the yard with overhead foliage. The spacious terrace echoes the curving lines of the lawn contours and makes a fine place for an outdoor party.

Besides feeding on the plentiful red, orange, and pink tubular-shaped flowers used in this design, the hummingbirds will make your yard practically insect free; they feed on tiny insects, snatching them from midair and collecting them from the flowers they visit. Avoid using pesticides, which will reduce the number of these insects, and perhaps directly harm the hummers.

Regionalized Plant Lists

Because climate and growing conditions vary greatly throughout North America, it is impossible to list here all the plants for this landscape plan that would do well everywhere on the continent. However, you can order a Blueprint Package with plant lists keyed to this plan and selected by expert horticulturists to thrive in your area.

The six-page Blueprint Package features a large-size version of this Plan View, plus a detailed regional Plant and Materials List. It also includes an illustrated list of hundreds of landscape plants suited to your region, in case you wish to make substitutions, as well as planting instructions and plant adaptation maps to ensure professional results with your new landscape.

See page 157 to order your regionalized Blueprint Package.

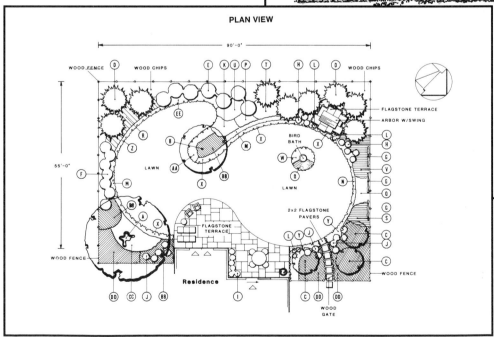

PLAN VIEW

Landscape Plan L274 shown in spring
Designed by Damon Scott

For swing and arbor plans, see page 149.

This pretty backyard plan provides the basics to attract hummingbirds—water and a spring-to-fall display of red, tubular-shaped, nectar-rich flowers. And this plan includes the amenities necessary for family comfort—a spacious patio, a shady swing, an attractive color scheme, and privacy plantings.

Songbird Garden

This naturalistic garden plan relies on several features to attract as many different species of birds as possible. A songbird's basic needs include food, water, and cover, but this backyard plan offers luxury accommodations not found in every yard, as well as the maximum opportunity for birds and bird watchers to observe each other. Special features cater to specific birds. For example, the rotting log attracts woodpeckers, and the dusting area will be used gratefully by birds to free themselves of parasites. In addition to the plentiful berries and seeds produced by the plants, there's a ground feeder that lures mourning doves, cardinals, and other birds that prefer to eat off the ground. The birdhouse (plans available separately) located in the shade of the specimen tree to the rear of the garden suits a wide variety of songbirds.

The angular deck (plans available separately) nestles attractively in the restful circular shapes of the garden. The designer enclosed the deck amid the bird-attracting plantings to maximize close-up observation opportunities and to create an intimate setting. Two other sitting areas welcome bird watchers into the garden. A bench positioned on a small patio under the shade of a graceful flowering tree provides a relaxing spot to sit and contemplate the small garden pool and the melody of a low waterfall. Another bench—this one situated in the sun—may be reached by strolling along a path of wood rounds on the opposite side of the yard. Both wildlife and people will find this backyard a very special retreat.

Regionalized Plant Lists

Because climate and growing conditions vary greatly throughout North America, it is impossible to list here all the plants for this landscape plan that would do well everywhere on the continent. However, you can order a Blueprint Package with plant lists keyed to this plan and selected by expert horticulturists to thrive in your area.

The six-page Blueprint Package features a large-size version of this Plan View, plus a detailed regional Plant and Materials List. It also includes an illustrated list of hundreds of landscape plants suited to your region, in case you wish to make substitutions, as well as planting instructions and plant adaptation maps to ensure professional results with your new landscape.

See page 157 to order your regionalized Blueprint Package.

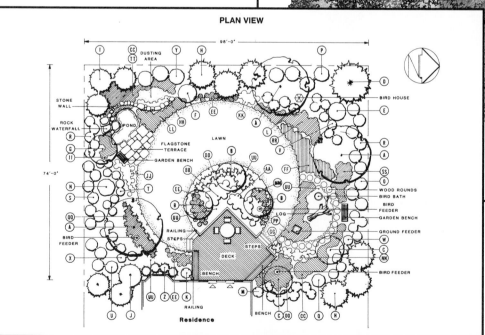

PLAN VIEW

Landscape Plan L275 shown in spring
Designed by David Poplawski

For Deck Plan D115, see page 152.
For birdhouse plans, see page 149.

This large, naturalistic backyard design creates a wonderful environment to attract a wide range of bird species, because it offers a plentiful supply of food, water, and shelter. The deck and garden benches invite people to observe and listen to the songbirds in comfort.

Springtime brings an extravaganza of bulbs to join the flowering trees in this garden, while summer and fall are filled with the blossoms of flowering perennials.

PICTURESQUE FLOWER GARDEN DESIGNS

Paint a Beautiful Flower Garden That Will Bloom For Months on End

If you've ever dreamed of having a breathtaking perennial garden—one brimming with colorful flowers from spring until frost—but don't know how to begin, the designs in this chapter are for you. Unlike the other landscape plans in this book, the four designs included here are for flower gardens only, not the entire backyard. You can incorporate one or more of these lovely gardens easily into your existing landscape. Two of the designs are unique lot-line treatments, created to run the length or width of the property. The other two, with vibrant color schemes, are island beds that fit any open spot in the yard.

These professionally designed flower gardens solve a lot of the planning problems for you. The designers carefully selected the flowers to create a colorful garden that's always exciting because it constantly changes. As one type of flower finishes its show for the season, another bursts into bloom. And the colors, sizes, and shapes of the flowers work together to create a beautiful garden picture—a picture painted by a talented artist using a palette of beautiful flowers.

ORCHESTRATING THE BLOOM

To keep a perennial garden exciting, designers know to include an assortment of plants that bloom in each of the major bloom periods: early to midspring, late spring to early summer, midsummer, late summer through early fall, and winter in mild climates. Do as the designers do by first creating a framework of three to five different types of plants to bloom during each period. For larger gardens, you can add additional flowers for each season or plant the garden to be especially showy during a particular season. Most gardeners enjoy a heavy bloom from June through August, because that's when they spend the most time outdoors. However, if you go away on vacation in midsummer, you may want a plentiful show in spring or fall.

Bulbs to Begin the Show

For a good display from early to midspring when few perennials blossom, include bulbs such as snowdrops, crocus, bluebells, daffodils, and tulips in the garden. Unfortunately, the foliage of these spring bloomers turns yellow and dies down by midsummer, leaving a bare spot in the garden. Garden designers often disguise this unsightly habit by interplanting perennials or annuals with bulbs. For example, by planting spring-blooming daffodils and summer-blooming daylilies in the same spot, the maturing daylily foliage grows up and around the withering daffodil leaves, creating a beautiful display of flowers twice a year in the same spot. Tulips can be lifted when their foliage yellows, and annuals can be planted in the same spot to carry on all summer.

Perennials and Summer Bulbs for the Main Show

Most perennials can be counted on to bloom for two or three weeks during a particular time from late spring to early fall, although some long-blooming types can perform for six to eight weeks. In planning a continuous sequence of bloom, a generous planting of these exceptionally long-blooming perennials provides good insurance against a lackluster garden devoid of blossoms.

Set off against attractive blue-green foliage, the small pink flowers of fringed bleeding-heart appear throughout the growing season. Golden-star, a good perennial for the shade, has yellow starlike flowers from May through October. Coreopsis 'Moonbeam' produces dainty pale yellow stars from midsummer to frost, and 'Goldsturm' coneflower presents dramatic golden black-eyed-susans from late summer to frost. Daylilies usually bloom for about four weeks, so by choosing a variety of early, midseason, and late cultivars, you can have daylilies in bloom from May through September.

Although the majority of bulbs bloom in early spring and midspring, some flower at other times. Lilies and gladiolus make a splashy display in the heat of summer. A few bulbs—autumn-crocus, colchicum, and sternbergia—even bloom in autumn.

Annuals For Continuity

Once annuals begin to flower in late spring or early summer, they usually continue to bloom right up until frost, as long as the faded flowers are regularly removed. Garden designers often arrange a few lavish patches of reliable annuals among the perennials to provide lasting color and continuity while the perennials go in and out of bloom.

The annuals can be changed from year to year to give the garden a different look. One year you may wish to plant white impatiens in the foreground, and the next year blue ageratum or lavender sweet alyssum.

Foliage Interest All Season

Look closer at a beautiful garden, and consider whether it's only the flowers that catch your attention. Although you rely on the flowers to provide splashes of color in the garden, plant foliage plays a major, although quiet, role. The textures and shapes of the leaves set off one plant from another. For example, the long, thin leaves of an ornamental grass contrast sharply with the leathery, round leaves of bergenia; the fernlike leaves of astilbe create a perfect foil for the flat, scallop-edged leaves of lady's-mantle.

When selecting neighboring perennials for your garden, consider not only how the flowers look together, but also how the foliage colors and textures

This curving island bed features a lovely collection of bright-flowered perennials that produce an ever-changing display of colorful blossoms from spring through fall.

combine. After all, the foliage endures in the garden much longer than the flowers. Many designers rely on plants with gray or silvery leaves or reddish bronze tones to provide an exciting contrast with green-leaved neighbors. Silver foliage looks especially lovely with blue or lavender flowers, and purple foliage combines well with pink blossoms.

DESIGN BASICS

In planting a perennial border that will be seen only from the front, divide the area roughly into three sections from front to back: foreground, midground, and background. Place the tallest plants in the background, medium ones in the midground, and low growers in the foreground, but avoid setting them in rigid rows. The garden will look more graceful if the plant heights weave in and out of each other a bit and if the flowers are placed in groups of the same type rather than planted polkadot fashion. Consider the height of the main mass of foliage, not the flower stems, when placing plants. Although the flower stalks can rise well above the foliage, they're transient, whereas the leaves remain all season.

In an island bed, the tallest plants go in the middle with lower ones on the perimeter, so you can view the garden from all sides. For the most aesthetically pleasing design, the tallest perennials in the background should be two-thirds the width of the border. The wider the border, the taller the background plants can be. For example, if the border is 3 feet wide, the tallest plants should be no higher than 2 feet high, but if the area were increased to 6 feet wide, the tallest plants could be up to 4 feet high. Midsize perennials, which range from 15 to 36 inches high, are the choices for the midground, whereas low-growing perennials, under 15 inches high, belong in the foreground.

The background forms the framework from which the rest of the garden is built. This is a good place for impressive ornamental grasses and tall spiky flowers, because they provide an interesting backdrop for lower-growing plants. The midground gives the border its character. It has a dual purpose: Not only does it relate to the plants behind it, but also it serves as the setting for the foreground. Especially in the midground, plants are most effective when placed in irregular drifts of three, five, or seven, rather than being planted individually. However, if an individual plant takes up a lot of space, one may be enough. A group of three suffices for large plants, whereas smaller plants should be used in larger numbers to achieve a comparable effect. Variety is important in the garden, so have three of one type of plant, five of another, and seven of yet another to create rhythm and interest.

Add the garden's finishing touches to the front third of the border. Study the garden as you've planted it so far, then try to balance any deficiencies with the plantings in the foreground. If the color seems a bit drab, jazz it up with some bright flowering plants here. Conversely, if it's too garish, tone it down by adding either white-flowering plants or gray or green foliage plants. Use creeping plants that form mats to tie the foreground together. A few well-chosen drifts of annuals placed in the foreground will help solve color problems and act as space fillers.

You may want to space out drifts of plants that bloom at the same time, so the color spreads over a wide area in the garden. Mixing colors, textures, flower shapes, and bloom times evenly throughout the garden creates the most interest.

Color Schemes

Beauty is in the eye of the beholder, especially when it comes to gardens. Some gardeners love a garden bursting in a rainbow of flowers, whereas others go to great lengths to create a garden with a sophisticated color scheme. But even gardeners who like a lot of color understand that not all floral colors combine well. For instance, orange-red clashes with purplish red but looks wonderful with blue and yellow. Salmon pink looks sick next to bright pink but works well with yellow and orange. Masses of white or cream-colored flowers or silver-foliaged plants help to separate warring colors.

Two of the gardens illustrated in this chapter follow precise color schemes: a red, white, and blue garden; and a yellow and blue garden. The other two don't follow obvious color schemes, although the designers chose the flowers carefully to blend a variety of colors into pleasing combinations.

CARING FOR YOUR PERENNIAL GARDEN

Once established, your perennial garden will need minimal care. Be sure to keep it well mulched to retain soil moisture, maintain fertility, and discourage weeds. Some tall perennials may need staking to keep them growing straight, and it's best to clip off faded flowers after the blooms are finished. Dried stalks should be cut off anytime between late fall and early spring before new growth commences. Since perennials increase in size, forming larger and larger clumps, most need to be dug up and divided every three to five years, although some, such as peony, gas plant, and wild indigo, stay healthy for years without division.

A lavish garden brings the drama of a continual parade of gorgeous flowers to your backyard. Not only will the garden appeal to your senses, but planning and planting it, and then nurturing and watching the plants develop and flower, provide a most pleasant hobby.

The English perennial border with its graceful masses of ever-changing flowers represents the epitome of fine perennial gardening. Planted in a corner of your property, this garden will provide enjoyment for years to come, since the designer filled it with an array of long-lasting, hardy plants.

English Perennial Border

The British, being renowned gardeners, boast the prettiest flower gardens in the world. Just the words *English perennial border* evoke instant images of masses of billowing blossoms, elegant hedges, and vine-draped thatched cottages. Their success in growing perennials to such perfection lies partly in the amenable British climate—cool summers, mild winters, plenty of moisture throughout the year, and very long summer days. Even without such a perfect climate, North American gardeners can achieve a respectable show of perennials by using plants better adapted to their climate. Arrange them into the flowing drifts made popular early in this century by British landscape designers, and you'll have the epitome of a perennial garden in your own backyard.

The perennial border shown here fits nicely into a corner of almost any sunny backyard. Pictured with a traditional evergreen hedge as a backdrop for the flowers, the garden looks equally lovely planted in front of a fence or house wall, as long as the area receives at least six hours of full sun a day.

The designer carefully selected an array of spring-, summer-, and fall-blooming perennials, arranging them in artful drifts for an ever-changing display. Spring and summer blooms paint a delightful pink, magenta, and pale yellow color scheme sparked here and there with splashes of white and blue, while autumn brings deeper colors—gold, dark pink, and purple. Patches of burgundy- and silver-hued foliage plants in the foreground help tie the elements of the garden together and play up the flower colors.

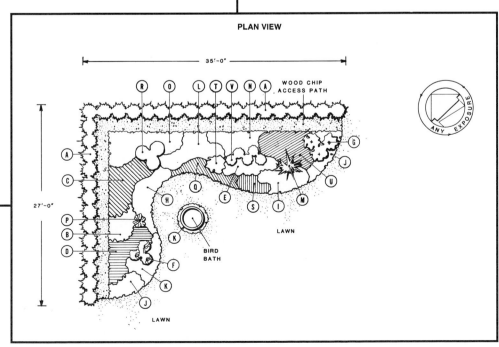

Landscape Plan L276 shown in summer
Designed by Michael J. Opisso

Regionalized Plant Lists

Because climate and growing conditions vary greatly throughout North America, it is impossible to list here all the plants for this landscape plan that would do well everywhere on the continent. However, you can order a Blueprint Package with plant lists keyed to this plan and selected by expert horticulturists to thrive in your area.

The six-page Blueprint Package features a large-size version of this Plan View, plus a detailed regional Plant and Materials List. It also includes an illustrated list of hundreds of landscape plants suited to your region, in case you wish to make substitutions, as well as planting instructions and plant adaptation maps to ensure professional results with your new landscape.

See page 157 to order your regionalized Blueprint Package.

129

Shady Flower Border

Y ou'll never again bemoan the fact that nothing will grow under the shade of the large trees in your backyard if you plant this beautiful shady flower border. Lawn grass needs full sun and struggles to grow under trees, so why not plant something that flourishes in the shade and looks a whole lot prettier! This charming flower border, featuring shade-loving perennials and ferns, fits under the existing trees along the property line of a shady backyard. Blooming from spring through fall, the border will delight you with its ever-changing display of flowers.

The garden floor features a low-spreading evergreen ground cover through which flowering perennials grow. The ground cover keeps the garden pretty the year around, even in winter when most perennials are dormant, and won't compete significantly with the flowering plants for nutrients or water. Large rocks and boulders also give the area year-round structure and interest, as does the bench, which invites you to sit and enjoy the pretty scene in the refreshing shade cast by the trees.

The designer chose to show this garden without a fence along the property border, but you could plant it in front of a fence, hedge, or other shrubbery and place it along any side of your yard. If your property isn't as large as the one shown here, the garden can easily be shortened by eliminating the corner containing the bench and ending the border with the grouping of rocks situated just to the left of the bench.

Regionalized Plant Lists

Because climate and growing conditions vary greatly throughout North America, it is impossible to list here all the plants for this landscape plan that would do well everywhere on the continent. However, you can order a Blueprint Package with plant lists keyed to this plan and selected by expert horticulturists to thrive in your area.

The six-page Blueprint Package features a large-size version of this Plan View, plus a detailed regional Plant and Materials List. It also includes an illustrated list of hundreds of landscape plants suited to your region, in case you wish to make substitutions, as well as planting instructions and plant adaptation maps to ensure professional results with your new landscape.

See page 157 to order your regionalized Blueprint Package.

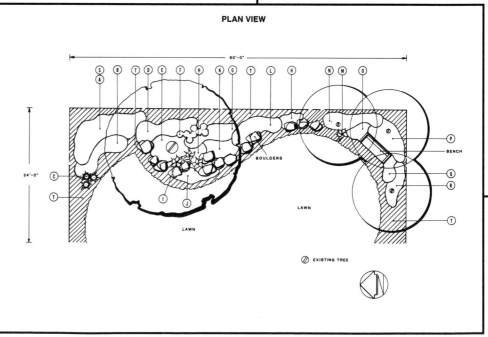

PLAN VIEW

Landscape Plan L277 shown in summer
Designed by Michael J. Opisso

This garden of shade-loving plants flourishes under trees where grass struggles to survive. Be sure to keep the plants healthy by providing plenty of water and fertilizer, especially if the garden plants compete for moisture and nutrients with thirsty tree roots. Thin out selected tree branches if the shade they cast is very dense.

Natural color companions, blue and yellow flowers create a pleasing garden scene that looks great anywhere it's planted. This island bed works perfectly in an open sunny yard, but it could be modified to fit along the side of a house or to back up against a fence or hedge along a property border.

Blue and Yellow Island Bed

Blue and yellow flowers planted together reward the gardener with a naturally complementary color scheme that's as bright and pretty as any garden can be. It's hard to err when using these colors, because the pure blues and the lavender blues—whether dark or pastel—look just as pretty with the pale lemon yellows as with the bright sulfur yellows and the golden yellows. Each combination makes a different statement, some subtle and sweet as with the pastels, and others bold and demanding as with the deep vivid hues. But no combination fails to please.

The designer of this beautiful island bed, which can be situated in any sunny spot, effectively orchestrated a sequence of blue- and yellow-flowering perennials so the garden blooms from spring through fall. The designer not only combined the floral colors prettily together, but incorporated various flower shapes and textures so they make a happy opposition. Fluffy, rounded heads of blossoms set off elegant spires, and mounded shapes mask the lanky stems of taller plants. Large, funnel-shaped flowers stand out against masses of tiny, feathery flowers like jewels displayed against a silk dress.

Although the unmistakable color scheme for this garden is blue and yellow, the designer sprinkled in an occasional spot of orange to provide a lovely jolt of brightly contrasting color. A few masses of creamy white flowers frost the garden, easing the stronger colors into a compatible union.

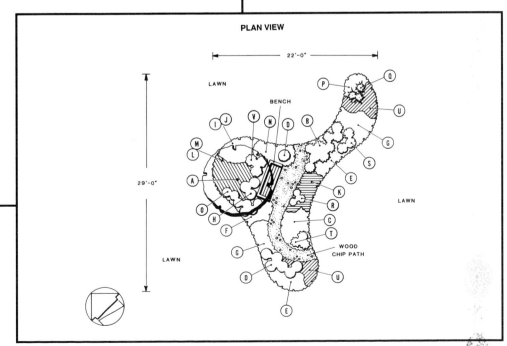

PLAN VIEW

22'-0"

29'-0"

LAWN

BENCH

LAWN

LAWN

WOOD
CHIP PATH

Landscape Plan L278 shown in summer
Designed by Damon Scott

Regionalized Plant Lists

Because climate and growing conditions vary greatly throughout North America, it is impossible to list here all the plants for this landscape plan that would do well everywhere on the continent. However, you can order a Blueprint Package with plant lists keyed to this plan and selected by expert horticulturists to thrive in your area.

The six-page Blueprint Package features a large-size version of this Plan View, plus a detailed regional Plant and Materials List. It also includes an illustrated list of hundreds of landscape plants suited to your region, in case you wish to make substitutions, as well as planting instructions and plant adaptation maps to ensure professional results with your new landscape.

See page 157 to order your regionalized Blueprint Package.

Red, White, and Blue Flower Garden

Let the colors of Old Glory shine in your yard with this red, white, and blue flower garden. Designed as a dramatic island bed to be planted in any open, sunny location in your yard, this versatile garden features combinations of flowering perennials and annuals carefully selected so the bed blooms from spring through fall in an ever-changing display of the colors of the flag. The long-blooming annuals, which should be planted in the spots where bulbs flowered in spring, provide a constant mass of color against which the perennials bloom in an exciting sequence.

Red can be a difficult color in the garden, since scarlet tones, with their hints of orange, clash terribly with crimson shades, with their hints of blue or purple. Likewise, blue comes in many tints, not all of which combine well with the various reds. White flowers separate and calm the strong blues and reds of this bold color scheme, giving the garden brightness and sparkle. The designer selected the flowers for their pure, bright colors, choosing ones that blossom in the red and blue tints that look great together and that will assuredly look superb when planted as the centerpiece of your backyard.

The designer planned the garden in a somewhat formal fashion, with blocks of plants laid out around a wood-chip path and central flagpole. The path affords you access to the flowers for easy planting and tending, while bringing you right into the garden where you can enjoy the flowers at close range.

Regionalized Plant Lists

Because climate and growing conditions vary greatly throughout North America, it is impossible to list here all the plants for this landscape plan that would do well everywhere on the continent. However, you can order a Blueprint Package with plant lists keyed to this plan and selected by expert horticulturists to thrive in your area.

The six-page Blueprint Package features a large-size version of this Plan View, plus a detailed regional Plant and Materials List. It also includes an illustrated list of hundreds of landscape plants suited to your region, in case you wish to make substitutions, as well as planting instructions and plant adaptation maps to ensure professional results with your new landscape.

See page 157 to order your regionalized Blueprint Package.

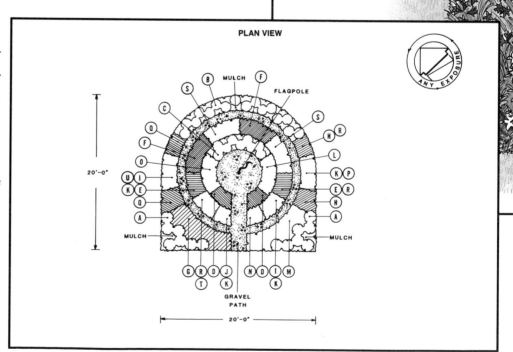

PLAN VIEW

Landscape Plan L279 shown in summer
Designed by Michael J. Opisso

The bold and dramatic color scheme of this island flower bed is further emphasized by the formal nature of the garden plan. Geometrically laid out in changing bands of flowers, the garden forms a dynamic centerpiece for any sunny yard.

An informal garden bursting with pretty flowers and graceful foliage creates a perfect setting for a Victorian cottage.

INSTALLING YOUR LANDSCAPE

Here's How to Adapt Any of These
Landscapes to Your Site

The plans in this book were designed to assist you in landscaping your backyard—making the landscape as beautiful, special, and livable as it can be. There are several ways the professionally designed plans included here can help to make your dream landscape a reality. If your yard and your family's needs match one of the designs in this book, you can use that design exactly or almost as it appears on the pages. Where slight variations in the size of your yard or in the layout of your home occur, you can easily adapt the plans—this chapter tells you how. Or you may want to follow the plans as a basic recipe, using your own imagination and creativity to customize a plan to your home.

If you've never designed a landscape, it's understandable that you may not feel comfortable about how to begin. You may be concerned that you lack the necessary creativity, knowledge, or experience. If this is in the back of your mind, don't worry, because you can quite easily adapt the designs presented in this book.

Study the plans and the renderings in Chapters 2 through 10, concentrating on the ones you think may look attractive on your property. Select the one with the landscaping style you like the most, and then proceed with any necessary adjustments as outlined in this chapter.

CHOOSING PLANTS TO CARRY OUT THE PLANS

The plans in this book indicate the layout and placement of plants and hardscape, but they don't detail the exact name or variety of plants used to carry out the design. This is because landscape plants are adapted to different climates, and very few are suited to all areas. For any of the plans featured here, you can order a complete set of blueprints with a plant list selected specifically to do well in your region (see page 154 to order). Or you can choose your favorite locally adapted plants to carry out the design. Even though the plans in this book don't indicate the exact plants to use, you can read the template (see illustration on page 139) to tell where the designer chose to place different types and sizes of trees, shrubs, ground covers, and perennials, so you won't go wrong.

The plan itself solves the design problems of artistically laying out the landscape by balancing sizes and shapes to complement the yard. The designer figured out where to locate outdoor living and recreation areas, and decided where and how to best direct people gracefully through the yard. This basic layout will remain the same regardless of the particular plants you choose to include—make sure, however, that the plants are in keeping with the spirit of the landscape design, as shown in the color illustration, and aren't likely to outgrow their allotted space.

CREATING YOUR BACKYARD PLAN

A drawing that accurately depicts the size, shape, and important features of your new landscape is an

Photo: David Goldberg

essential requirement before installing a landscape design. There is no other way to test—before planting—whether a tree, once mature, will be too close to the house, or a shrub will crowd a walk. The process of making the drawing also tends to generate ideas, and certainly it's quicker to experiment with a pencil and an eraser than with a shovel and your muscles. The time you spend putting your plan on paper pays off later.

Plan-Making Tools

You'll need tracing paper, pencils, an eraser, a scale ruler, and several large sheets of graph paper. You can find graph paper in various sizes, but 18- by 24-inch sheets are the most useful because they're the same size as the blueprints for the plans in this book. Although a triangular-shaped scale ruler isn't essential, you'll find that it makes measuring to scale much quicker. To make your plan as professional looking as possible, you may also want to have handy a T-square, template of landscape symbols, and compass.

Begin With a Survey

You'll need an accurate drawing of your existing backyard. The best way to start is with your official property survey. If you didn't get a copy when you purchased the property, your city building department should have one on file. If not, you'll need to measure the property boundaries yourself or have the land professionally surveyed.

Draw your plot plan using a convenient scale—usually 1 inch of drawing representing either 4 or 8 feet of property. If the scale is too compressed, less than ⅛ inch to the foot (⅛ scale), details become smaller and more difficult to visualize. On the other

hand, if the scale is too large, the plan may not fit on the paper.

If you plan to order a set of blueprints for one of the plans shown in this book, you'll find it convenient to use the same scale as the plans you get. Plans of large properties employ a scale of 1 inch for 8 feet (same as ⅛ inch for 1 foot) and those of smaller properties use a scale of 1 inch for 4 feet (same as ¼ inch for 1 foot).

On tracing paper accurately redraw your survey, enlarging it to fit the chosen scale. Then add all existing and permanent features that you want to keep, such as pathways, a patio or deck, and walls. Next draw in all existing trees, shrubs, and garden areas that you want to keep. This will be easy for a newly built home on an otherwise empty property. Once you've included these permanent landscape features on the plot plan, note the locations of all doors and windows. Don't guess at the dimensions. Use a 50- or 100-foot tape measure and work as precisely as you can. Finally, using a directional arrow, mark which way is north. Once your drawing is complete, have it photocopied so that the original is kept safe and clean while you experiment with the copies to your heart's content.

Now you're ready to design the new landscape for your backyard. If you're adapting a plan from this book, use a scale ruler to enlarge it to fit the same scale as your existing plot plan. If you're starting with landscape blueprints, you won't need to redraw anything.

Lay the tracing-paper copy of your existing landscape over the blueprints or enlarged tracing of the landscape plan from the book and see how good a fit you have. Place another piece of tracing paper on top of the two drawings—you can use small pieces of tape to keep the sheets aligned—and then begin to make adjustments in the layout, if necessary.

MAKING THE FIT: ADAPTING THE PLAN TO YOUR BACKYARD

Most likely, any plan in this book won't fit your backyard exactly—almost, but not exactly. (The designs were created to fit typical backyards for either ¼-, ⅓-, or ½-acre properties.) If your property varies from these sizes, that shouldn't be a major problem, because a few professional tricks will allow you to adapt the plans to a larger, smaller, or differently shaped yard. Here's how to do it: Tape a new sheet of tracing paper over both your present plot plan and the backyard design you wish to adapt. Trace only the permanent features and dimensions of your present backyard onto the new sheet of paper. Then undo the tape, remove the tracing of the existing plot and shift the new paper over the plan that you wish to adapt, tracing the design's prominent features in slightly different locations. Here are some examples of how to make specific adjustments.

Adjusting for Different Lot Sizes and Shapes

Your property may be a bit longer, narrower, or larger than the average-sized properties for which these designs are created. If you intend to use one of these basic designs on a larger property, there are several options available. Where the property line is farther to the left, keep the planting bed on the left the same size and simply redraw it along the edge of the property line, making up for the difference by increasing the size of the lawn. It's more economical to widen the lawn area than increase the number of shrubs. You can also make the planting bed slightly deeper, but not so deep that it's hard to maintain or is out of scale with the rest of the design.

To use any of these designs on a much larger property, you may choose to keep the planting beds just about where they're shown in the plan and use a backdrop of tall evergreen trees for additional privacy. Moving a planting bed over to the left or right to accommodate a larger property often leaves a gap in the planting. Fill in this gap at a suitable point, such as where it curves around toward the house, by adding more plants of the same type; for example, plant five yews instead of three. Where even larger areas need to be filled in, repeat an entire group of plantings, which may include another tree of the same type along with additional shrubs and more ground covers and perennials.

A professional designer doesn't regard the lawn area as a catchall to solve leftover space, and neither should you. The size and shape of the lawns on these plans represent an important part of the overall design. The lawn acts as a sculptural element; it guides views and circulation around the property. Maintain the shape of the lawn and its relationship

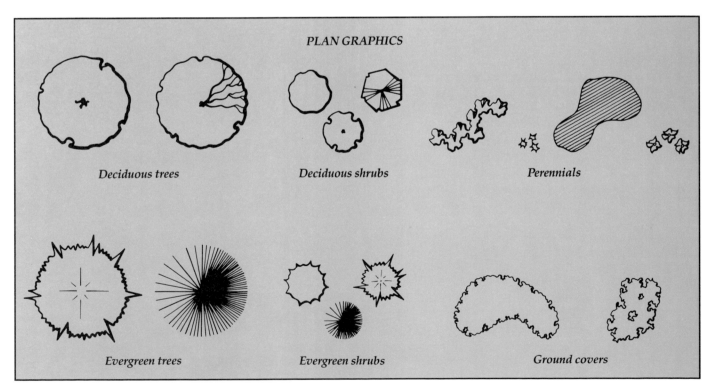

The graphic symbols shown here are ones commonly used on professional landscape designs to indicate different types of plants. Size varies to indicate the plants' mature sizes.

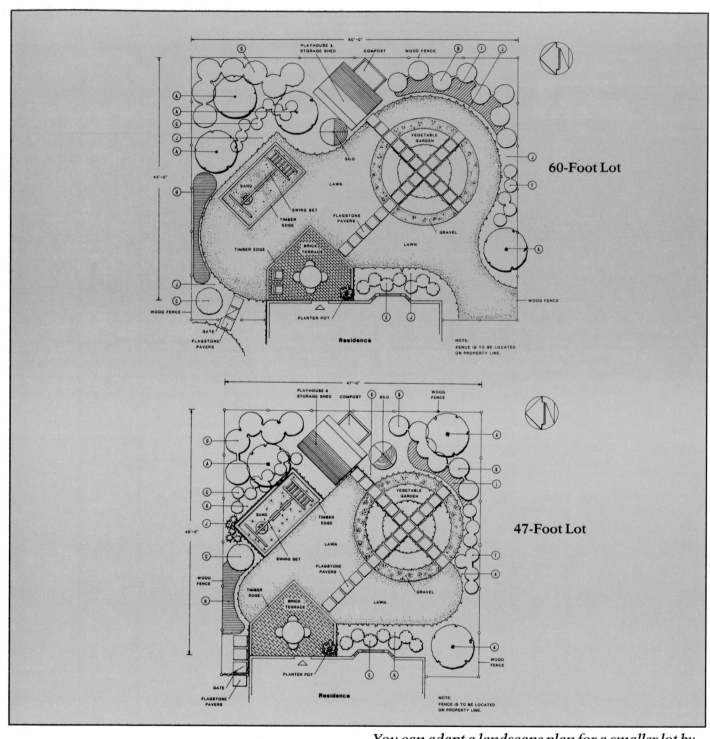

60-Foot Lot

47-Foot Lot

You can adapt a landscape plan for a smaller lot by judiciously eliminating one or more of a group of plants and rearranging other features to create a compact version of the original design. The plan for the Children's Vegetable Garden (L255) pictured on top was created for a 60-foot-wide lot. The version pictured on the bottom shows how this was adapted to a 47-foot-wide lot by eliminating several trees, repositioning a few shrubs, and eliminating some of the lawn.

with the rest of the plantings as much as possible when making adjustments in scale. This may mean enlarging island beds or including an additional tree or two to maintain balance on a larger property; conversely, on a smaller property you may wish to scale down the size of island beds and remove one or more trees from a group.

When you're reducing the size of a lawn, keep in mind that a turf area less than 6 to 8 feet wide serves little design purpose and is difficult to maintain. In such an instance, substitute a ground cover or paving for the lawn. Large trees and shrubs that border a lawn area will be out of proportion if the size of the lawn is greatly reduced. When this occurs, substitute smaller trees and shrubs in place of the larger ones to scale down that portion of the design. Conversely, increasing the size of the lawn significantly calls for larger trees and shrubs at the perimeter.

It's not difficult to adjust a larger design to a smaller piece of property. For instance, if the distance to the right side of the property line from the house is smaller than on the plan, include only one tree with its underplantings where three are indicated, and make the lawn area smaller as necessary.

You can remove a shrub grouping entirely to reduce the size of a plan, or you can take out several plants from each group of shrubs and perennials

along the width or depth of the property to adjust the design. Professional designers usually work with odd numbers of plants. You may see one specimen tree or a planting of three, five, or seven shrubs, but you'll rarely see two, four, or six of a particular plant. When making adjustments, follow professional design techniques and expand or contract the planting by working with odd numbers.

Adjusting for a Different House Layout

Are you saying "I like the backyard design but my house has a wing on the other side"? Or perhaps, "The sliding doors from the dining room face the other direction"? Most differences in house layout can easily be accommodated to your design using the tracing-paper technique.

If your house is a mirror image of one shown here, the solution is simple: Trace the plot plan and then flip the paper over. *Voilá*, you have an instant landscape plan!

Whenever an adjustment is made for a different house layout, remember that the professional designer used certain principles when creating the landscape plan. Any adjustments you make must be done with those principles in mind. Any changes to one side will need balancing changes on the other side. Remember, too, that balance doesn't necessarily

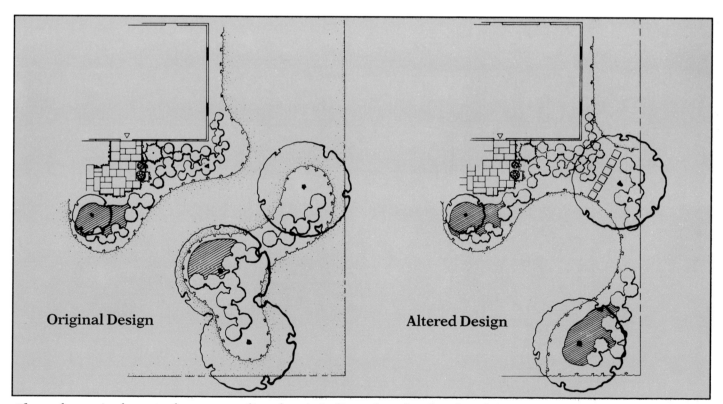

Original Design

Altered Design

If your house is closer to the property line than is indicated on the plot plan, it is an easy matter to adapt the design to fit your lot. The original design (left) employs three trees and an island bed to the side of the yard. The altered design (right) uses the same plants but rearranges them to fit the smaller space by eliminating one of the trees and some of the shrubs and extending the ground cover bed into an appealing arc.

mean symmetry. If you're not sure how to accomplish this, you may want to consult a professional designer.

Adjusting Plans to a Sloped Property

The landscapes illustrated in Chapters 2 and 3 were created for relatively flat pieces of property or for properties with a slight slope away from the house. If your property is more sloped, you can adjust many of these plans to fit either by regrading or by working with the existing terrain and adding a series of steps and landings or even retaining walls. A change of grade involves more than just aesthetics. Rather than a professional designer, you may require an engineer or licensed contractor to assure that changing the grade doesn't create drainage problems.

ADJUSTING FOR GRADING AND DRAINAGE

Sometimes it seems that the grass really is greener on the other side. People who live where the land is flat find it dull and uninteresting, and often they go out of their way to create height and contours in the garden. People who live on a sloped property often try to flatten it out so they can play volleyball or avoid having the problem of getting up the driveway when it's covered with ice and snow.

Even a property that seems flat may not really be perfectly flat. Almost every property has some grade (slope) or dips and rises. The grade of a property shouldn't be confused with grading, which is the term used to describe changing the existing slope. You should assess the variations in grade on your property and consider any necessary or desired grade changes before finalizing your landscape design.

Grading needs may be minimal or extensive. You may need to flatten an area for a patio or a ground-level deck. Your lawn may need grading so that it slopes evenly away from the house toward the street. Some plans call for adding mounds of earth, known as berms, for effectively screening a view or adding interesting height to an otherwise flat property. Changes of grade can also be used to separate one activity area of the landscape from another.

The grade shouldn't be changed around the drip line of a large tree because this can either expose or bury the roots, eventually killing the tree. If it becomes necessary to raise the grade around a tree, construct a well around it to avoid burying the roots.

Drainage Considerations

Grading and drainage are interdependent. It's best to grade your property so that water drains away from structures and doesn't collect in beds, borders, and paved areas. Proper grading prevents having to

Landscape design: Ireland-Gannon Associates

This attractive stone retaining wall, while creating two flat areas where the ground once sloped, provides year-round interest and a perfect backdrop for displaying flowers and foliage.

pump water out of the basement after heavy rains. It eliminates low areas where water and snow collect instead of draining away properly. Water should drain quickly from paved areas so the pavement doesn't become an icy hazard or remain unusable for hours after a rainstorm.

Paved areas should maintain a minimum pitch of ⅛ inch per foot, but ¼ inch is better. A patio that's located next to the house should slope away slightly from the structure. If the patio is located in a lower part of the landscape, where water can't run off because a wall or higher ground surrounds the paving, then you'll need drains and drain pipes to channel water away. Discuss the matter with a professional designer to ensure a practical and economical solution.

It's wise to know how well your soil drains before you plan any grade changes. You can use a simple method that professionals employ for testing drainage. Dig a hole 2 feet deep by any width; you can dig a narrow hole with a posthole digger if the soil is hard. Fill the hole with water and let it drain for a day, then fill it again. If it's empty or less than one-third full the following day, there is no drainage problem. If it's still two-thirds or more full, the drainage problem is severe, and you may need to install drainage pipes or tiles. If the hole is between one-third and two-thirds full, you may be able to correct the drainage problem by amending the soil.

Consider your soil structure. Will changing the grade expose areas with poor soil and bury good topsoil? It may be necessary to change grade in a two-step process. You may have to remove the topsoil and hold it in reserve, do the grading, and then replace the topsoil. You may also need to purchase soil to complete a grading project—a decision that will affect your budget. Soil is expensive, so try to fill in low areas of your property by moving soil from a higher level. Any soil that you purchase should be as close as possible in texture and composition to the existing soil. Placing a fast-draining soil over a heavy, poor-draining soil will cause a subsurface drainage problem that may drown the plants growing above. Removing trees and shrubs when you change the grade may also alter the drainage pattern, sometimes for the better, sometimes not.

Consultation with utility companies may be necessary to determine the location of underground pipes and cables. Proposed changes in grade may be impossible if the pipes and cables will be exposed or if access to them or their meters will be blocked.

You shouldn't just move soil around the garden or pave large areas without first thinking of the consequences. Before attempting any major changes in grade or before paving large areas near the house, consult a professional to ensure that your plan won't cause drainage problems. A professional can help you determine whether some type of drainage tiles or pipes need to be installed, or how to change the grade to avoid potential problems.

If your property is relatively flat and the soil is naturally fast draining, you needn't be seriously concerned about drainage. Follow the principles outlined for changing grade to ensure that any new structures or paved areas have proper drainage. On the other hand, if you have heavy soil, consult a professional regarding the installation of drainage pipes.

INSTALLING THE LANDSCAPE

Whether you plant the shrubs and trees and construct the walkways and the deck or patio yourself, or hire a contractor to do all or part of the work, there are several things to consider.

Construction Regulations

Many communities have building codes that may affect how you install your landscape. City building and planning departments create these rules for good reasons, primarily to ensure the safety of current and subsequent owners, and to maintain the community's attractive appearance. It's your responsibility to find out which, if any, regulations govern your backyard plans.

If you're planning to install new plants only, you probably won't need a permit, although the height of shrubs, walls, and fences at the property line may be restricted in some situations. Permanent structures and home improvements, such as decks, patios, and retaining walls, may require building permits. The city will require proof of proper engineering, and, in most cases, it may demand that such structures be a certain distance from the property line. Swimming pools almost always require enclosure by fence to prevent small children from accidentally wandering into the area.

Transferring Your Plan

Once you've cleared the area to be landscaped, transfer your plan to your property. Using a measuring tape, accurately measure the location of all new walkways, structures, and plants. Place markers to indicate areas of major construction, such as a deck, a pool, or walkways. Mark the sites of major trees and the outline of planting beds and borders. You can use wood or metal stakes and run strings between them to show clearly where everything will be located. A garden hose or a clothesline works well to outline beds and borders.

Stand on the site of the proposed deck and double-check the location and the views. Note if trees are properly located. Walk from the side of the house to the various doors to make sure the walkways are in the most logical place. Walk out to the gate or side yard and see what a first-time visitor will see. Go inside and look at your landscape from indoors. When you're pleased with all aspects of the design, then you can start to put your plan into action.

PLANTING YOUR BACKYARD LANDSCAPE

In most cases, thorough soil preparation before planting is essential for the ongoing health of plants. The best way to start is with a soil test. Contact your local County Extension Service or a private soil-testing laboratory. Along with the results will come detailed recommendations on how to improve your soil. They will most likely include an addition of organic matter, such as composted fir bark or sawdust. Spread 2 or 3 inches of the organic material over the soil where you've indicated the planting beds and till it in. Additional fertilizer, and perhaps lime or sulfur to adjust the soil pH, may also be specified.

Removing Lawn

There are several ways to remove an existing lawn where new beds and borders, walkways, or a patio will go. The lawn can be stripped away just below the roots with a spade, or you can rent a power sod cutter. Sod that's stripped off can be saved and transplanted where it's needed. If you have no need for the sod, use it as fill or add it to the compost pile. When building a ground-level deck, don't bother removing the lawn under it, because the grass will soon die from lack of light. Lawns can also be killed with an herbicide such as glyphosate, but be careful not to spray the chemical accidentally on desirable plants, or you'll kill them, too.

If you're removing an existing lawn and installing a new lawn in the same area, take advantage of the

When starting a new planting bed where lawn is growing, first strip off the sod with a spade, then turn over the soil. This prevents the grass from returning as weeds.

Balled-and-burlapped shrubs are easy to plant. **Top left:** *Dig a hole larger and wider than the rootball. Improve the backfill by mixing in peat or compost, returning some soil to the bottom of the hole.* **Top right:** *Place the plant in the hole so it is level with the soil surface.* **Bottom left:** *Fold back the burlap, fill the hole part way and water.* **Bottom right:** *Fill hole to the top, gently press the soil in place, then form a ring of soil over the rootball to hold water.*

situation and improve the soil. Both seeded and sodded lawns will be healthier and need less care for years to come if the soil has been amended. Till organic matter into the soil and level the ground. Roll the surface after seeding or sodding. Keep the newly planted lawn moist until it's well established.

Planting Trees and Shrubs

Trees and shrubs are available as dormant bare-root, balled-and-burlapped (B&B), or container-grown plants. Both bare-root and B&B plants are grown in native soil in nursery fields. Bare roots are dug while they're dormant and the soil is washed off. Since they're quite perishable, they should be planted promptly. B&B plants are similarly field grown and dug up, but the soil surrounding the root ball is retained and wrapped with burlap or a synthetic fabric. B&B plants can survive for weeks before planting, but it's wise to keep them shaded and moist. Bare-root plants are best planted in late winter, and B&B plants in early spring or fall soon after they're dug up.

Container-grown plants can be installed anytime without suffering transplant shock, since their root systems are completely intact. Before removing a plant from its container, check to see if the soil is moist. If not, water the plant thoroughly and allow it to drain. When it's moist—not dry or soggy—it's much easier to handle and less prone to fall apart. Hold the plant upside down or lay it sideways on the ground, and gently let it fall or slide out of the container. Set the plant in the hole and check its height: To allow for soil settling, make sure the plant is slightly higher than it was in the container. If the

roots are matted or circling, loosen them, heading them outward, before refilling the hole. Backfill halfway, apply water, then finish backfilling.

Newly planted trees and shrubs can suffer greatly from a lack of water, since they haven't yet rooted into the surrounding soil. To help retain water and direct it to roots, make a ring or berm of raised soil around the plant and flood the basin periodically with water. After planting, apply an organic mulch, such as wood chips, over the soil to keep it moist.

Planting Ground Covers and Lawns

Many ground covers are sold in flats or packs, the same as most flowering annuals. Space them uniformly—usually five pachysandra, three English ivy, or three ajuga plants for every square foot. For quicker coverage, plant closer together; to save money, plant farther apart, although the plants will take longer to fill in.

Start a new lawn with either seeds or sod. A seeded lawn costs less but requires more attention until it gets established. If the lawn area is greater than about 1,500 square feet, the savings gained by using seeds instead of sod are substantial. Sod costs more initially but looks great right away. Where the lawn is relatively small, the difference in actual cost is small. The most important decision for you to make about a lawn is which variety of grass to plant: Consult a knowledgeable nursery or your county agent about the best grass varieties for your climate. Usually a mixture of several types is best, because a mix resists disease better than a single variety.

You can install sod yourself or have it done professionally. Sod comes in several standard widths based on the size of the cutting tool, but the thickness should be between ½ and 1 inch—thicker pieces may not establish well. Sod often comes stacked or rolled, but it shouldn't be kept this way for more than 24 hours because heat buildup can injure the grass. After delivery, unroll or unstack the pieces and lay them in the shade if you can't plant them immediately. Be sure to keep them moist.

Prepare the soil by tilling in organic matter. Rake it smooth and level, and water before planting the sod. Begin by installing the sod along the longest edge of the area to be sodded. Lay the pieces in a staggered bricklike pattern, butting the ends together. Use a serrated knife to cut pieces to fit curves. As you work, it's best to walk on a board laid across the sod to prevent the pieces from slipping.

Once the sod is laid, roll it at right angles with a heavy roller to press the roots into the soil. New sod requires watering several times a week for the first month or two. You can mow as soon as the lawn needs it, but don't fertilize until the next season.

The best time to sow seeds is early spring or fall; fall sowing is usually more successful in any climate. You can sow successfully in winter in some warm climates, and you probably get away with it in summer in some cool climates if you water adequately. Prepare the soil as described above, then spread seeds evenly across the soil using a drop spreader. Divide the total amount of seeds needed by half and spread them by walking across the area twice, making the second pass at right angles to the first. (The rate of seeding—number of pounds of seeds per 100 square feet—varies with grass variety.) Roll the soil to press the seeds into the soil. Using a light mist that won't wash away the seeds, water every day to keep the soil surface moist until the seeds germinate—about ten days. Continue watering regularly until the grass is established.

HIRING A LANDSCAPE CONTRACTOR

The virtue of the plans offered in this book is that you can enjoy the benefits of a professional design without paying the cost of custom work. Many handy do-it-yourselfers can easily manage the variety of tasks required in installing a landscape; others may wish to hire a landscape contractor to carry out

Once the work is done, be sure to provide your new outdoor living space with suitable furniture where you can relax and admire the beautiful landscape you created.

some or all of the installation. You may wish to do the planting and contract the brickwork or decking, or vice versa.

A landscape contractor isn't by definition a designer. A contractor knows how to follow blueprints, plant trees and shrubs, build retaining walls, and the like. Rarely are landscape contractors skilled landscape designers, although they may offer to design a landscape. They may be able to purchase the landscape plants at a reduced cost to you if you hire them to install the landscape, thus offsetting some of the cost of their work.

Ask your friends and neighbors for recommendations for a contractor and ask to see examples of work. Ask each prospective contractor for cost and scheduling estimates. Don't neglect to compare lists of materials and their relative quality when making your choice. Once you've decided on an individual, write out a contract that specifies work and payment schedules. Under no circumstances should you post a construction bond for a contractor. Keep copies of all plans, building permits, certificates of occupancy, and inspections after the work is completed. You'll need them when you sell the house.

When your backyard landscape is finished, the property will have a beautiful look that you and your family will enjoy for years to come. The new backyard will improve your outdoor living environment the day it's completed, and the initial investment will more than pay for itself over the years by continuing to add to the increasing value and comfort of your home.

PLANS FOR GARDEN STRUCTURES
Three-Bin Composter

FRANK FRETZ

If compost is food for the soil, then consider a compost bin the oven. With the right amount of moisture and sufficient oxygen, regulated in a well-designed unit, organic matter will heat quickly and decompose thoroughly.

A covered bin helps keep the compost moist while keeping out excess moisture. Side-by-side bins allow you to scoop and transfer layers from one bin to the next, effectively "turning" the pile and supplying it with oxygen. Three compartments provide space for continuous composting: Two bins are used for processing, and the spare bin for collecting.

Each bin of our composter holds 27 cubic feet of organic materials — the ideal size for making quick compost. Open the hatch and toss kitchen and yard waste into the "holding bin." Remove the front slats a few at a time (for working in an existing pile) or all at once (for forking layers from one bin to the next). The bin rests on a sturdy base and includes a floor.

PROCEDURE FOR BINS

Base. Nail a header to each end of the center floor joist, using 16d nails. Nail the outside joists, front and back, across the ends of the headers. Nail the brace blocks in place between the joists. Locate and nail the four short floorboards across the joists where the partitions will be located, using 8d nails, as shown.

Partitions. For each of the four partitions (two outside and two inside), nail six partition boards to connect two corner posts. Nail the inside door tracks to the partition boards, 1 inch back from the front corner posts.

ILLUSTRATIONS BY CARSON ODE

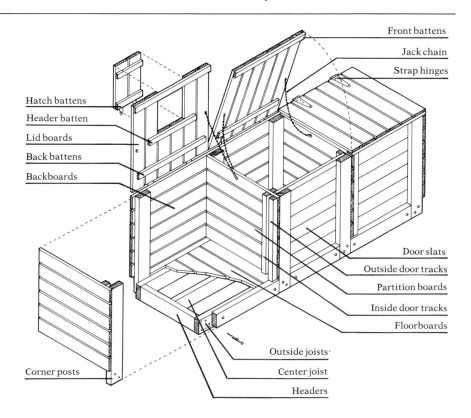

Front battens
Jack chain
Strap hinges
Hatch battens
Header batten
Lid boards
Back battens
Backboards
Door slats
Outside door tracks
Partition boards
Inside door tracks
Floorboards
Corner posts
Outside joists
Center joist
Headers

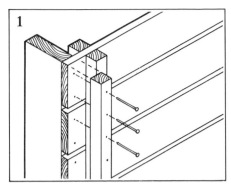

Nail the outside door tracks flush with the front of the two interior partitions. Position the assembled partitions — one on each end of the base and one on each side of the interior compartment; drill and bolt the corner posts to the outside joists.

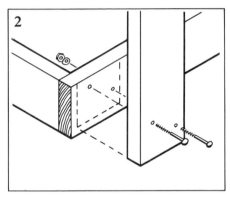

Post Blocks. Cut the 2 x 6 into three pieces, to fit snugly between the bottoms of the front corner posts. Bolt the post blocks in place, flush with the floor surface.

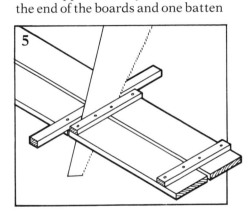

Floor. Nail the floorboards in place across the joists. (There will be five for each of the two end compartments and four for the middle compartment.)
Back. Nail the backboards in place, covering back-corner posts.
Front. Feed door slats horizontally into door tracks.

PROCEDURE FOR LIDS

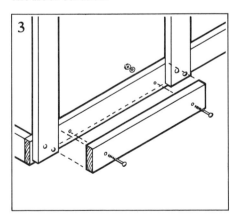

Lids. Construct two of the three lids. Using a drill and galvanized screws, fasten six lid boards to the front and back battens; allow approximately ½ inch between boards. Each lid will measure 36 inches across. Construct the third lid in the same manner, but leave out the two middle boards.
Hatch. Fasten the hatch battens to the two remaining lid boards, one batten approximately 2 inches from the end of the boards and one batten

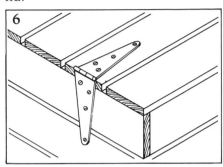

18 inches from the same end. Fasten the header batten to the boards, 20 inches from the end, just behind the back-hatch batten. Cut between the header batten and the back-hatch batten to separate the hatch. Fasten the two remaining boards and header batten to the partially constructed lid. Hinge the hatch to the lid.

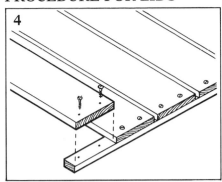

Finish. Hinge the three lids to the bins with the 8-inch hinges, so that they are centered over the compartments. Attach a chain to the bottom of both end lids, at about the middle of the end boards, with screw eyes. Attach a chain to the bottom of both middle-lid end boards, as shown. Mount snap hooks on the ends of the chains. Use pliers to attach screw eyes to the bin partitions, as shown.

Editor's Note: If you prefer, use untreated pine rather than pressure-treated lumber. Paint with a low-toxicity preservative, such as copper naphthenate.

MATERIALS FOR BINS

LUMBER*
1 pc. 2 x 6 x 108″ (center joist)
2 pcs. 2 x 6 x 30″ (headers)
2 pcs. 2 x 6 x 111″ (outside joists)
2 pcs. 2 x 6 x 14¼″ (brace blocks)
4 pcs. 1 x 6 x 33″ (short floorboards)
8 pcs. 2 x 6 x 41½″ (corner posts)
24 pcs. 1 x 6 x 36″ (partition boards)
6 pcs. 2 x 2 x 34″ (inside door tracks)
2 pcs. 2 x 2 x 35½″ (outside door tracks)

1 pc. 2 x 6 x 96″ (cut to fit for post blocks)
14 pcs. 2 x 6 x 34½″ (floorboards)
6 pcs. 1 x 6 x 111″ (backboards)
18 pcs. 1 x 6 x 35½″ (door slats)
3 pcs. 1 x 3 x 35½″ (door slats)
HARDWARE
22 carriage bolts ¼ x 3½″ with nuts and washers
1 box galvanized nails 16d
1 box galvanized nails 8d

MATERIALS FOR LIDS

LUMBER*
18 pcs. 1 x 6 x 37″ (lid boards)
3 pcs. 1 x 2 x 36″ (front battens)
3 pcs. 1 x 2 x 34″ (back battens)
2 pcs. 1 x 2 x 11¼″ (hatch battens)
1 pc. 1 x 2 x 22″ (header batten)
HARDWARE
6 strap hinges 8″ (lids)
2 strap hinges 4″ (hatch)

4 lengths jack chain, approx. 36″ each
8 heavy screw eyes
4 snap hooks
1 box galvanized screws #6 x 1¼″
TOOLS
Electric drill
Saw (jigsaw or handsaw)
Hammer
Pliers

147

Sun Designs

Sun Designs publishes books and plans for a wide variety of products made from wood. These products range from Gazebos, Backyard Structures, Cupolas, and Bridges, to children's toys such as Wagons, Sleighs, Rocking Horses, and other wooden objects. The designs on the following pages provide interesting and practical ways to add exciting amenities to your favorite backyard plan.

For more information on obtaining construction drawings for the plans shown — or for information on the full line of plan books available — call, write or fax:

Sun Designs
P.O. Box 676
Whitewater, WI 53190

TOLL FREE 1-800-765-0176
FAX 414-473-6112

Minaret Gazebo
Layout: 6-side hexagon shape
Size: 9' 2" point to point
Height: 15' 6" ground to top

Sentinel Gazebo
Layout: 6-side hexagon shape
Size: 9' 2" point to point
Height: 14' 9" ground to top

Carouselle Gazebo
Layout: 8-side octagon shape
Size: 13' 0" point to point
Height: 18' 9" ground to top

Holiday Strombella
Layout: Rectangular shape
Size: 11' 10" x 5' 6"
Height: 8' 0" ground to top

Fairfax Swing
Layout: Rectangular shape
Size: 3′ 6″ x 5′ 8″
Height: 8′ 2″ ground to top

Greenwood Arbor
Layout: Rectangular shape
Size: 12′ 0″ x 10′ 0″
Height: 9′ 0″ ground to top

Sumida Bridge
Length: 12′ 0″
Width: 4′ 0″
Weight capacity: 15 people

Mourning Dove Feeder
Type: Open feeder
Size: 11″ x 11″
Height: 14″

Warbler Birdhouse
Type: Enclosed house
Size: 29″ x 29″
Height: 42″

Bluebird Feeder
Type: Feeder with glass
Size: 10″ x 10″
Height: 11″

Walpole Woodworkers

Walpole offers a large variety of standard garden and storage buildings that can be modified to the owner's special requirements. By copying your architectural style, Walpole can create buildings to blend with your home, complete with such special details as multi-pane windows, shutters, cupolas, and flower boxes. No other small building company can offer you more choices.

All buildings are pre-assembled in sections and can be installed easily following instructions sent in the kit. Standard sections are joined by bolts and can be com-bined in a variety of sizes. The following small buildings are but three examples of the exclusive line of finely detailed, architect-designed structures that Walpole can supply in standard kit form or customized to your needs. For more information, contact:

Walpole Woodworkers, Inc.
767 East Street   **508-668-2800**
Walpole, MA 02081   **FAX 508-668-7301**
(Eleven other locations in Massachusetts, Connecticut, and New York)

Salt Box
Layout: Rectangular shape
Size: 6' 0" x 8' 0"
Height: 7' 4" ground to roof ridge
Features: Salt box roof, split-entry door, single 6-lite window with shutters and flower box

Fancy Salt Box
Layout: Rectangular shape
Size: 8' 0" x 10' 0"
Height: 7' 10" ground to roof ridge
Features: Salt box roof, cupola, circlehead split-entry door, single 6-lite circlehead window with shutters and scallop shingles

New England Salt Box
Layout: Rectangular shape
Size: 8' 0" x 15' 0"
Height: 8' 8" ground to roof ridge
Features: New England salt box roof, cupola, circlehead door, twin 8-lite windows with shutters and flower boxes

18'-0"

14'-0"

PLAY ROOM
7⁴ X 9⁴

BUNK ROOM
5⁸ X 6⁴

LADDER

LOFT ABOVE

BUNK BED

LADDER

PORCH

TRELLIS
ABOVE

14'-0"

10'-0"

PLAY ROOM
BELOW

BUNK ROOM
BELOW

RAILING

TRAP
DOOR

LOFT
7⁴ X 5⁴

Children's Playhouse From Home Planners

Make a child's playhouse dream come true with this whimsical scaled-down house by Conni Cross. It has its own wraparound front porch with a trellis covering and a real front door leading to the main play area. The attached bunk room with built-in beds provides space for sleep-overs. Three windows in the play room and one in the bunk room provide plenty of natural light for reading and playing. Reached through a trap door in the ceiling is a loft area that overlooks the play room below. This area is also enhanced with natural light. A delightful play center for any child!

Complete construction blueprints and materials list are available. See page 156 to order.

Conni Cross, designer
Cutchogue, New York

151

Home Planners' Deck Plans You Can Build

A beautiful deck addition can mean so much, not only to the value of your home but also to the enjoyment you and your family will share while using this outdoor extension. On these two pages are three deck additions you can actually build or have a professional contractor build for you. Each of the decks is easily adaptable for any style or size of home and offers special details such as the tri-levels of D119 and the built-in seating offered by D115 and D120.

Complete construction blueprints are available for each of the decks (to order see page 156). The blueprint packages include everything you or your contractor will need for the deck project — frontal sheet, materials list, floor plan, framing plan, and deck elevations. A Standard Deck Details package for building *any* deck is also available.

Deck Plan D115

KITCHEN-EXTENDER DECK

Although not a large expanse, just over 525 square feet, this stylish deck makes use of angles and strategic placement to create a sense of spaciousness and room extension. Indoors, a large country kitchen features dual sliding doors opening onto the deck, making the kitchen more accessible to the outdoors.

This design is also distinguished by its contemporary wedge shape, and could be a problem-solving design for a small or odd-shaped lot.

Built-in benches provide extensive seating — enough for fairly large gatherings. The railing is bolstered by privacy-creating latticework. One set of intricately designed stairs "V" outward to ground level, helping guide users, while providing a custom touch to this simple yet highly functional deck.

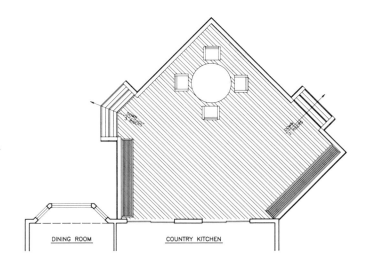

DINING ROOM   COUNTRY KITCHEN

TRI-LEVEL DECK WITH GRILL

This deck offers the best of both worlds. With three levels totaling over 650 square feet and an elongated shape, it is well-suited for simultaneous activities without disturbing the participating parties. Stairways are not required to go from one level to the next: The deck is thoughtfully designed so that each level has a change in elevation equal to a step. The result is a deck composed of three separate areas, made even more distinctive by contrasting surface patterns for each area.

The geometric angles of the deck's perimeter add interest and allow some unique features, such as the large, three-sided bench that wraps around one extended deck section. In addition, a moveable grill is installed near the kitchen door for barbecues. The grill can also be built as a wet bar. Planters add a finishing touch. Access to the ground level is via two exits: one near the kitchen, the other outside the covered porch.

Deck Plan D119

CONTEMPORARY LEISURE DECK

A contemporary design is just one attribute of this diminutive yet appealing deck. An overall feeling of spaciousness is achieved in a small area (550 square feet) due to the creative changes in angle and space. This design would work extremely well in an odd-shaped lot, or where existing trees or other landscape features require some ingenuity and imagination to achieve a good "fit."

Benches are built in between matching planters in an area outside of the living room for an intimate seating arrangement. The deck extends outward dramatically to create a large area outside of the family room, with plenty of space for table and chairs. Railing surrounds the deck for a finishing touch, as well as for safety. A simple, single step down provides access to ground level in three different corners of the deck.

Deck Plan D120

153

Ordering Landscape Plans

The Landscape Blueprint Package

The Landscape Blueprint Package available from Home Planners includes all the necessary information you need to lay out and install the landscape design of your choice. Professionally designed and prepared with attention to detail, these clear, easy-to-follow plans offer everything from a precise plot plan and regionalized plant and materials list to helpful sheets on installing your landscape and determining the mature size of your plants. These plans, together with the information in Chapter 11 on adapting the design to your lot, will help you achieve professional-looking results, adding value and enjoyment to your property for years to come.

Each set of blueprints is a full 18" x 24" in size with clear , complete instructions and easy-to-read type. Consisting of six detailed sheets, these plans show how all plants and materials are put together to form an exciting landscape for your home.

Frontal Sheet. This artist's line sketch shows a typical house and all the elements of the finished landscape when plants are at or near maturity. This will give you a visual image or "picture" of the design and what you might expect your property to look like when fully landscaped.

Plan View. Drawn at 1/8" equals 1'-0", this is an aerial view of the property showing the exact placement of all landscape elements, including symbols and callouts for flowers, shrubs, ground covers, walkways, walls, gates, and other garden amenities. This sheet is the key to the design and shows you the contour, spacing, flow, and balance of all the elements in the design, as well as providing an exact "map" for laying out your property.

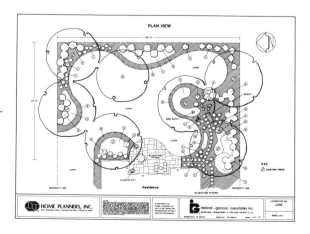

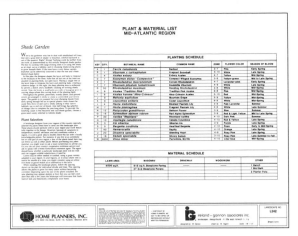

Regionalized Plant & Materials List. *Keyed to the Plan View sheet, this page lists all of the plants and materials necessary to execute the design. It gives the quantity, botanical name, common name, flower color, season of bloom, and hardiness zones for each plant specified, as well as the amount and type of materials for all driveways, walks, walls, gates, and other structures. This becomes your "shopping list" for dealing with contractors or buying the plants and materials yourself. Most importantly, the plants shown on this page have been chosen by a team of professional horticulturalists for their adaptability, availability, and performance in your specific part of the country.*

Planting and Maintaining Your Landscape. *This valuable sheet gives handy information and illustrations on purchasing plant materials, preparing your site, and caring for your landscape after installation. Includes quick, helpful advice on planting trees, shrubs and ground covers, staking trees, establishing a lawn, watering, weed control, and pruning.*

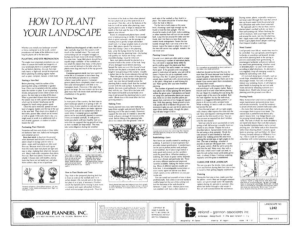

Zone Maps. *These two informative maps offer detailed information to help you better select and judge the performance of your plants. Map One is a United States Department of Agriculture Hardiness Zone Map that shows the average low temperatures by zones in various parts of the United States and Canada. The "Zone" listing for plants on Sheet 3 of your Plant and Materials List is keyed to this map. Map Two is a Regional Adaptation Map which takes into account other factors beyond low temperatures, such as rainfall, humidity, extremes of temperature, and soil acidity or alkalinity. Both maps are key to plant adaptability and are used for the selection of landscape plants for your plans.*

Plant Size & Description Guide. *Because you may have trouble visualizing certain plants, this handy regionalized guide provides a scale and silhouettes to help you determine the final height and shape of various trees and shrubs in your landscape plan. It also provides a quick means of choosing alternate plants appropriate to your region in case you do not wish to install a certain tree or shrub, or if you cannot find the plant at local nurseries.*

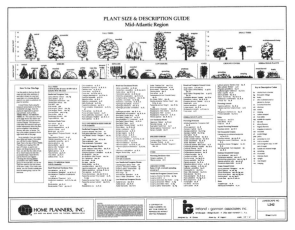

To order, see page 157.

Plans Price Schedule and Index

To order your plans, simply find the Plan Number of the design of your choice in the Plans Index below. Consult the Price Schedule below to determine the price of your plans, choosing the 1-, 3-, or 6-set package and any additional or reverse sets you desire. To make sure your Plant & Materials List contains the best selection for your area, refer to the Regional Order Map below and specify the region in which you reside. Fill out the Order Coupon on the opposite page carefully and mail to us for prompt fulfillment or call our Toll-Free Order Hotline for even faster service.

Landscape Plans Price Schedule

Price Group	W	X	Y	Z
1 set	$25	$35	$45	$55
3 sets	$40	$50	$60	$70
6 sets	$55	$65	$75	$85

Additional Identical Sets ....$10 each
Reverse Sets (Mirror Image) ....$10 each

Deck Plans Price Schedule

Price Group	Q	R	S
1 set	$25	$30	$35
3 sets	$40	$45	$50
6 sets	$55	$60	$65

Additional Identical Sets ....$10 each
Reverse Sets (Mirror Image) ....$10 each

Landscape Plans	Page	Price	Available For Regions:
L240	107	Y	ALL
L241	74	Y	ALL
L242	38	Y	ALL
L243	108	Z	ALL
L244	24	Y	ALL
L245	119	Y	ALL
L246	81	Z	ALL
L247	64	Z	ALL
L248	62	Z	ALL
L249	111	Y	ALL
L250	88	Y	ALL
L251	90	Z	ALL
L252	54	Y	ALL
L253	42	Z	ALL
L254	92	Z	ALL
L255	26	Y	ALL
L256	28	Y	ALL
L257	30	X	ALL
L258	37	Z	1-3, 5, 6, 8
L259	40	Y	ALL
L260	45	Z	1-3, 5, 6, 8
L261	50	Y	1-6, 8
L262	53	Y	ALL
L263	57	Z	1-3, 5-8
L264	67	Z	ALL

Landscape Plans	Page	Price	Available For Regions:
L265	68	Z	ALL
L266	76	Y	ALL
L267	79	Z	ALL
L268	82	Y	ALL
L269	94	Y	ALL
L270	97	Z	ALL
L271	102	Y	ALL
L272	104	Y	ALL
L273	117	Z	ALL
L274	120	Z	ALL
L275	122	Z	ALL
L276	129	W	ALL
L277	130	W	ALL
L278	133	W	ALL
L279	134	W	ALL

Deck Plans	Page	Price
D115	152	Q
D119	153	R
D120	153	S

Plan	Page	Price
Children's Playhouse	151	$30

Regional Order Map

Region 1 **Northeast**
Region 2 **Mid-Atlantic**
Region 3 **Deep South**
Region 4 **Florida & Gulf Coast**
Region 5 **Midwest**
Region 6 **Rocky Mountains**
Region 7 **Southern California & Desert Southwest**
Region 8 **Northern California & Pacific Northwest**

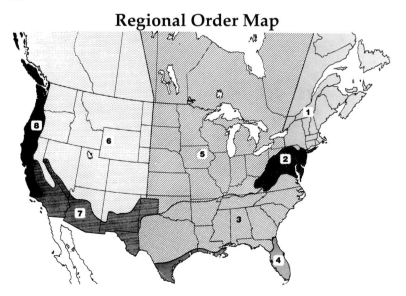

Blueprint Order Form

To order, just clip the accompanying order blank and mail with your check or money order. If you prefer, you can also use a credit card or order C.O.D. (Sorry, no C.O.D. shipments to foreign countries, including Canada.) If time is of essence, call us Toll-Free at 1-800-521-6797 on our Blueprint Hotline. If your call is received by 5:00 p.m. Eastern Time, we'll ship your order the next business day. If you use the coupon, please include the correct postage and handling charges.

Our Exchange Policy
Because we produce and ship plans in response to individual orders, we cannot honor requests for refunds. However, you can exchange your entire order of blueprints, including a single set if you order just one, for a set of another landscape or deck design. All exchanges carry an additional fee of $15.00, plus $5.00 for postage and handling if they're sent via surface mail; $7.00 for priority air mail.

About Reverse Blueprints
If you want to install your landscape or deck in reverse of the plan as shown, we will include an extra set of blueprints with the Frontal Sheet and Plan View reversed for an additional fee of $10.00. Although callouts and lettering appear backwards, reverses will prove useful as a visual aid if you decide to flop the plan.

How Many Blueprints Do You Need?
To study your favorite landscape or deck plan or make alterations of the plan to fit your site, one set of Blueprints may be sufficient. On the other hand, if you plan to install the landscape or build the deck yourself using subcontractors or have a general contractor do the work for you, you will probably need more sets. Because you save money on 3-set or 6-set packages, you should consider ordering all the sets at one time. Use the checklist below to estimate the number you'll need:

Blueprint Checklist
____Owner
____Contractor or Subcontractor
____Nursery or Plant Materials Supplier
____Building Materials Supplier
____Lender or Mortgage Source, if applicable
____Community Building Department for Permits
(sometimes requires 2 sets)
____Subdivision Committee, if any
____Total Number of Sets

Blueprint Hotline
Call Toll-Free 1-800-521-6797. We'll ship your order the following business day if you call us by 5:00 p.m. Eastern Time. When you order by phone, please be prepared to give us the Order Form Key Number shown in the box at the bottom of the Order Form.

CANADIAN CUSTOMERS:
Order Toll-Free 1-800-848-2550. Or, complete the order form above, and mail with your check indicating U.S. funds to:
Home Planners, Inc.,
3275 W. Ina Road, Suite 110,
Tucson, AZ 85741

HOME PLANNERS, INC.,
3275 WEST INA ROAD, SUITE 110
TUCSON, ARIZONA 85741

Please rush me the following Blueprints:

_____ Set(s) of Landscape Plan _____.
(see Index and Price Schedule) $_____

_____ Set(s) of Deck Plan _____. $_____

_____ Additional identical blueprints
in same order @ $10.00 per set. $_____

_____ Reverse blueprints @ $10.00 per set. $_____

_____ Standard Deck Details @ $14.95 per set. $_____

_____ Children's Playhouse @ $30.00. $_____

Please indicate the appropriate region of
the country for Plant & Material List
(See Map on opposite page):
❑ Region 1   Northeast
❑ Region 2   Mid-Atlantic
❑ Region 3   Deep South
❑ Region 4   Florida & Gulf Coast
❑ Region 5   Midwest
❑ Region 6   Rocky Mountains
❑ Region 7   Southern California & Desert Southwest
❑ Region 8   Northern California & Pacific Northwest
SALES TAX (Arizona residents add 5% sales tax;
Michigan residents add 4% sales tax.) $_____

POSTAGE AND HANDLING		
UPS DELIVERY-Must have street address - No P.O. Boxes		
•UPS Regular Service Allow 4-5 days delivery	❑ $5.00	$_____
•UPS 2nd Day Air Allow 2-3 days delivery	❑ $7.00	$_____
•UPS Next Day Air Allow 1-2 days delivery	❑ $16.00	$_____
POST OFFICE DELIVERY If no street address		
•Priority Air Mail Allow 4-5 days delivery	❑ $7.00	$_____
C.O.D. (Pay mail carrier; Available in U.S. only)	❑ Send COD	

TOTAL IN U.S. FUNDS $_____

YOUR ADDRESS (please print)

Name _____

Street_____

City _____ State _____ Zip _____

Daytime telephone number (_____)_____

FOR CREDIT CARD ORDERS ONLY

Please fill in the information below:

Credit card number _____

Exp. Date: Month/Year _____

Check one: ❑ Visa ❑ MasterCard ❑ Discover Card

Signature _____

Order Form Key

Additional Plans Books

THE DESIGN CATEGORY SERIES

1.

ONE-STORY HOMES
A collection of 470 homes to suit a range of budgets in one-story living. All popular styles, including Cape Cod, Southwestern, Tudor and French. **384 pages. $8.95 ($10.95 Canada)**

2.

TWO-STORY HOMES
478 plans for all budgets in a wealth of styles: Tudors, Saltboxes, Farmhouses, Victorians, Georgians, Contemporaries and more. **416 pages. $8.95 ($10.95 Canada)**

3.

MULTI-LEVEL AND HILL-SIDE HOMES 312 distinctive styles for both flat and sloping sites. Includes exposed lower levels, open staircases, balconies, decks and terraces. **320 pages. $6.95 ($8.95 Canada)**

4.

VACATION AND SECOND HOMES 258 ideal plans for a favorite vacation spot or perfect retirement or starter home. Includes cottages, chalets, and 1-, 1½-, 2-, and multi-levels. **256 pages. $5.95 ($7.50 Canada)**

THE EXTERIOR STYLE SERIES

9.

330 EARLY AMERICAN HOME PLANS A heartwarming collection of the best in Early American architecture. Traces the style from Colonial structures to popular traditional versions. Includes a history of different styles. **304 pages. $9.95 ($11.95 Canada)**

10.

335 CONTEMPORARY HOME PLANS Required reading for anyone interested in the clean-lined elegance of Contemporary design. Features plans of all sizes and types, as well as a history of this style. **304 pages. $9.95 ($11.95 Canada)**

11.

COLONIAL HOUSES 161 history-inspired homes with up-to-date plans are featured along with 2-color interior illustrations and 4-color photographs. Included are many plans developed for *Colonial Homes'* History House Series. **208 pages. $10.95 ($12.95 Canada)**

12.

COUNTRY HOUSES Shows off 80 country homes in three eye-catching styles: Cape Cods, Farmhouses and Center-Hall Colonials. Each features an architect's exterior rendering, artist's depiction of a furnished interior room, large floor plans, and planning tips. **208 pages. $10.95 ($12.95 Canada)**

PLAN PORTFOLIOS

MOST POPULAR HOME DESIGNS
Our customers' favorite plans, including one-story, 1 ½-story, two-story, and multi-level homes in a variety of styles. Designs feature many of today's most popular amenities: lounges, clutter rooms, media rooms and more.

14. 272 pages. $8.95 ($10.95 Canada)

AFFORDABLE HOME PLANS For the prospective home builder with a modest or medium budget. Features 430 one-, 1½-, two-story and multi-level homes in a wealth of styles. Included are cost saving ideas for the budget-conscious.

15. 320 pages. $8.95 ($10.95 Canada)

LUXURY DREAM HOMES At last, the home you've waited for! A collection of 150 of the best luxury home plans from seven of the most highly regarded designers and architects in the United States. A dream come true for anyone interested in designing, building or remodeling a luxury home.

16. 192 pages. $14.95 ($17.95 Canada)

NEW FROM HOME PLANNERS

5.

WESTERN HOME PLANS
Over 215 home plans from
Spanish Mission and Mon-
terey to Northwest Chateau
and San Francisco Victorian.
Historical notes trace the
background and geographi-
cal incidence of each style.
**208 pages. $8.95 ($10.95
Canada)**

6.

DECK PLANNER 25 practical
plans and details for decks the
do-it-yourselfer can actually
build. How-to data and project
starters for a variety of decks.
Construction details available
separately. **112 pages. $7.95
($9.95 Canada)**

7.

THE HOME LANDSCAPER
55 fabulous front- and backyard plans that even the do-it-
yourselfer can master. Complete construction blueprints
and regionalized plant lists
available for each design. **208
pages. $12.95 ($15.95 Canada)**

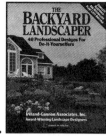

8.

BACKYARD LANDSCAPER
Sequel to the popular *Home
Landscaper*, contains 40 professionally designed plans for
backyards to do yourself or
contract out. Complete construction blueprints and
regionalized plant lists
available. **160 pages. $12.95
($15.95 Canada)**

13.

VICTORIAN DREAM HOMES 160
Victorian and Farmhouse designs by
three master designers. Victorian style
from Second Empire homes through
the Queen Anne and Folk Victorian
era. Beautifully drawn renderings
accompany the modern floor plans.
192 Pages. $12.95 ($15.95 Canada)

17.

**NEW ENCYCLOPEDIA OF HOME
DESIGNS** Our best collection of plans
is now bigger and better than ever!
Over 500 plans organized by architectural category including all types and
styles and 269 brand-new plans. The
most comprehensive plan book ever.
352 pages. $9.95 ($11.95 Canada)

Please fill out the coupon below. We will process your order and ship it from our
office within 48 hours. Send coupon and check for the total to:

HOME PLANNERS, INC.
3275 West Ina Road, Suite 110, Dept. BK
Tucson, Arizona 85741

THE DESIGN CATEGORY SERIES — A great series of books edited
by design type. Complete collection features 1376 pages and
1273 home plans.

1. ____ One-Story Homes @ $8.95 ($10.95 Canada)	$ _____
2. ____ Two-Story Homes @ $8.95 ($10.95 Canada)	$ _____
3. ____ Multi-Level & Hillside Homes @ $6.95 ($8.95 Canada)	$ _____
4. ____ Vacation & Second Homes @ $5.95 ($7.50 Canada)	$ _____

NEW FROM HOME PLANNERS

5. ____ Western Home Plans @ $8.95 ($10.95 Canada)	$ _____
6. ____ Deck Planner @ $7.95 ($9.95 Canada)	$ _____
7. ____ The Home Landscaper @ $12.95 ($15.95 Canada)	$ _____
8. ____ The Backyard Landscaper @ $12.95 ($15.95 Canada)	$ _____

THE EXTERIOR STYLE SERIES

9. ____ 330 Early American Home Plans @ $9.95 ($11.95 Canada)	$ _____
10. ____ 335 Contemporary Home Plans @ $9.95 ($11.95 Canada)	$ _____
11. ____ Colonial Houses @ $10.95 ($12.95 Canada)	$ _____
12. ____ Country Houses @ $10.95 ($12.95 Canada)	$ _____
13. ____ Victorian Dream Homes @ $12.95 ($15.95 Canada)	$ _____

PLAN PORTFOLIOS

14. ____ Most Popular Home Designs @ $8.95 ($10.95 Canada)	$ _____
15. ____ Affordable Home Plans @ $8.95 ($10.95 Canada)	$ _____
16. ____ Luxury Dream Homes @ $14.95 ($17.95 Canada)	$ _____
17. ____ New Encyclopedia of Home Designs @ $9.95 ($11.95 Canada)	$ _____
Sub-Total	$ _____
Arizona residents add 5% sales tax; Michigan residents add 4% sales tax	$ _____
ADD Postage and Handling	$ 3.00
TOTAL (Please enclose check)	$ _____

Name (please print) _____

Address _____

City _____ State _____ Zip _____

CANADIAN CUSTOMERS: Order books
Toll-Free 1-800-848-2550. Or, complete the
order form above, and mail with your check
indicating U.S. funds to: Home Planners, Inc.,
3275 W. Ina Road, Suite 110, Tucson, AZ 85741.

**TO ORDER BOOKS BY PHONE
CALL TOLL FREE 1-800-322-6797**

TB24BK

INDEX